SMUGGLING LIGHT

ESTHER CHANG
WITH EUGENE BACH

SMUGGLING LIGHT

WHITAKER
HOUSE

Publisher's Note:
Names, places, and dates have been altered to protect those still living and serving in China and North Korea.

All Scripture quotations are taken from *The Holy Bible, English Standard Version,* © 2000, 2001, 1995 by Crossway Bibles, a division of Good News Publishers. Used by permission. All rights reserved.

Smuggling Light:
One Woman's Victory over Persecution, Torture and Imprisonment

Eugene Bach
BacktoJerusalem.com

ISBN: 978-1-62911-792-8
eBook ISBN: 978-1-62911-793-5
Printed in the United States of America
© 2016 by Back to Jerusalem, Inc.

Whitaker House
1030 Hunt Valley Circle
New Kensington, PA 15068
www.whitakerhouse.com

Library of Congress Cataloging-in-Publication Data

Names: Chang, Esther, 1967– author. | Bach, Eugene, 1976– author.
Title: Smuggling light : one woman's victory over persecution, torture, and imprisonment / Esther Chang with Eugene Bach.
Description: New Kensington, PA : Whitaker House, 2016.
Identifiers: LCCN 2016039078 (print) | LCCN 2016042244 (ebook) | ISBN 9781629117928 (trade pbk. : alk. paper) | ISBN 9781629117935 (E-book)
Subjects: LCSH: Chang, Esther, 1967– | Missionaries—Korea (North)—Biography. | Missionaries—China—Biography. | Missions—Korea (North)—History. | Missions—China—History.
Classification: LCC BV3462.C43 A3 2016 (print) | LCC BV3462.C43 (ebook) | DDC
266.0092 [B] —dc23
LC record available at https://lccn.loc.gov/2016039078

2 3 4 5 6 7 8 9 10 11 12 **W** 24 23 22 21 20 19 18 17

Contents

Prologue

Near the border of North Korea and China.
About eight years ago.

Hello?"

Esther answered the phone uncertainly. Although she recognized the number, she could never be sure who was on the other end. She always tried to pretend confusion until she was positive the caller wasn't the police.

"Esther," said a desperate voice. "Please help! I've been shot!"

Then the line went dead.

Esther immediately recognized the voice: it was Peter, a North Korean she had been discipling for over two years. She pressed the phone to her ear for a full thirty seconds in case the call was reconnected, but she heard nothing but silence.

———

Peter was one of the many North Koreans who illegally cross the Tumen and Yalu rivers into China in order to buy food and earn money to support their families. The rivers are heavily guarded on both the North Korean side and the Chinese side, and border guards often shoot first and ask questions later.

To cross without being seen, Peter would lie in the field by the river during the day and remain as still as possible, moving only a few inches per hour so that he would not draw any attention to himself. During the black of night, when he was least likely to be spotted, Peter would move faster through the bush until he got to the edge of the river. Once at the riverbank, he would take off his clothes, slowly slide into the icy water, and slip across in the darkness while holding his clothes above his head to keep them dry. He knew it was dangerous, but he also knew that if he didn't go back and forth to China, he and his whole family might die of starvation.

Either way, he was risking his life.

On this particular night, everything was proceeding as planned. Once he reached the Chinese side of the river, Peter was going to call the only person he knew could help him—Esther. She had been the first person to tell him about Jesus and he had come to saving faith through her ministry. She had spent several months training him at her home. She had also given him money, food, clothing, blankets, a mobile phone, audio Bibles, and video players containing *The Jesus Film* to bring back to his village. Once, Esther had even managed to recruit three former American servicemen to help smuggle him back into North Korea. But after distributing all the audio Bibles to the people in his village and using up all of the food and money, Peter needed to make another trip to China.

As he approached the Chinese bank, Peter suddenly heard a soldier yell out in the darkness. Because of the echo over the water Peter could not tell which direction the yells were coming from, but he knew he had been spotted. He moved faster through the frigid waters, rushing to get to the China side so he could hide in the forest. As soon as he made it to the frozen riverbank, a shot rang out. He whipped his head around in time to see a flash from the muzzle of a rifle before a searing pain bit into his leg. Wounded but alive, he managed to crawl into the forest and call Esther.

———

Several miles away, Esther was worried. There was no way she could have predicted this sudden turn of events. She prayed for Peter as she wrapped herself in a shawl to go find him.

"Where are you going, mom?" her son asked. Esther didn't know how to answer. She didn't know where to look for Peter, how she would find him, or what to do if she did. But her mind began forming vivid images of Peter lying in a field somewhere, bleeding from a gunshot wound, and she knew he needed her help now more than ever.

"Where are you going?" her son asked again.

"I am not sure. Just stay here with your grandmother," she said as she swooped out the door and waited for a taxi.

At the same time as Esther was getting into a taxi, the Chinese border guards were already closing in on Peter.

Because so many North Koreans attempt to cross the border into China every year, the border guards have become very skilled in tracking them down, like hunters honed from years of sporting. In fact, the Chinese authorities view refugee-hunting as one of the best ways to break in a rookie border guard. New guards are often forced to stand the longest portions of duty during the early morning hours. If they are unsuccessful in spotting illegal border crossings, they are punished at the end of the week. However, whichever rookie captures the most "illegals" is declared the winner for the week and is allowed to make fun of the other guards while on duty.

The tragedy is that these border guards are not hunting animals. They make a game of hunting starving human beings who are harmless and merely looking for a way to survive. Even worse, these refugees are usually easy to shoot and capture once spotted because their severely malnourished state causes them to move lethargically.

Peter was no different. They found him soon after he had called Esther. He was immediately arrested and forced to walk to the nearest road even though his leg was severely wounded.

At the road a police officer was ready to take him to the main jail just outside Tumen City. "Did you search him?" one of the police officers asked the border guard before taking Peter into custody.

"He's a bag of bones. What could he possibly be carrying?" the border guard snapped back, showing that he didn't have to answer to the police.

"It doesn't matter. Procedure must be followed. Who knows what these dogs might have?" the officer retorted as he began to search Peter. He pulled out Peter's mobile phone from an inside pocket and shoved it in Peter's face. "Who have you been talking to?"

The officer looked through the calls and redialed Peter's most recent number. Esther picked up the phone on the other end. "Hello? Peter? Where are you?"

In a whispering voice, the officer replied coolly, "Is this you?" He had evidently done this many times before.

"Yes, it is me. This is Esther. Where are you?" She paused. Something didn't seem right. There was a long silence on the line.

"Where are you now?" the officer asked in a whisper.

Esther realized it was not Peter on the phone. She hung up, but knew that the damage had been done.

"It's her!" exclaimed the police officer.

"Who?" asked the border guard.

"Esther! We have been looking for this woman for years!"

He was right. Esther had just been released from Chinese prison after being charged with human trafficking of North Koreans. But a few nights ago, her name had come up again when the Chinese police arrested a North Korean assassin. It turned out that China wasn't the only country hunting Esther.

The North Korean government has long attempted to solve the problem of Chinese Christians who live on the border of North Korea and are sympathetic to the plight of North Korean refugees. As the refugees sneak out of North Korea in droves to find food and money in China, they have learned that homes with crosses on their doors are places of refuge. Through the brave acts of the Chinese believers, large numbers of North Koreans have been coming to faith in Christ for decades.

One of the worst of these Chinese Christian offenders, in the eyes of the North Korean government, was Esther. They had imprisoned her before (as had the Chinese) and were planning to execute her. No one was certain why she was released, but the North Korean government was determined not to let that happen again.

They had even gone as far as to hire an assassin who traveled to China and attempted to infiltrate Esther's circle of Christian workers in order to find out who her contacts were. He was ordered to then kill everyone involved by stabbing them, one by one, with a syringe filled with poison. However, the assassin's plot was discovered when he was accidentally arrested in China on unrelated charges and the Chinese police found a list of names on him. He was tortured until he gave up the information they were looking for and that is when the Chinese government discovered he had been sent to kill Esther. That aggravated the Chinese police because it was proof she was once again illegally aiding these refugees—or as they called it, human trafficking.

After Esther hung up the phone with the police officer, she knew she and her family were in grave danger yet again. She had just been released from prison, so if she was arrested again, she would surely be executed or given a life sentence of hard labor, which is almost the same thing. She knew she had to dispose of the phone, find a new way to contact her family, and go on the run.

As she sat in the taxi, Esther left everything in God's hands. She was a wanted criminal in China and still the main target of a North Korean government assassination plot.

Following Jesus had put her in prison in both China and North Korea, but He had also led her out. Only Jesus could help her now.

CHAPTER 1

Part of a Third Culture

But now thus says the LORD, *he who created you, O Jacob,
he who formed you, O Israel: "Fear not, for I have redeemed
you; I have called you by name, you are mine."*
—Isaiah 43:1

Upon arrival to a certain small rural village on the border of China and North Korea, a visitor would immediately notice how different it is from anywhere else in China. With a local population made up of primarily Chinese-born Koreans, the village's signs and billboards are all written in both Korean and Chinese. Korean culture is a part of the village's everyday life. To the dismay of visiting Chinese, many local taxi drivers and waitresses speak only Korean when conducting business transactions. It is actually possible to live in this region without ever having to study the Chinese language.

The Korean-Chinese who live in this area are fully Chinese citizens, but are distinctly set apart from the Han Chinese majority and are one of China's many ethnic minorities. The food, language, cultural ceremonies, and customs in this region of China are all uniquely Korean. Yet, at the same time, these Korean-Chinese have also embraced their Chinese identity, seen most dramatically in the large number of Korean-Chinese soldiers who lost their lives while fighting for China in the Korean War. Their involvement in the war gained them great respect from both the Chinese and North Korean governments alike. In many ways the Korean-Chinese are not fully Chinese, nor fully Korean. They are in essence a third culture, a blend that contains elements of both.

Esther Chang

In 1967, a little girl was born into this unique village who would be used greatly by God for His work. Her name was Esther. And as will be seen, her third culture identity plays a vital role in the evangelization of North Korea today.

The 60s were a difficult era to be born in China. The Cultural Revolution was still in full swing. The ruler Mao Zedong had started the Revolution to prevent any possible drift toward capitalism. Through an intense propaganda campaign, China's youth were led to declare war on the "four olds," zealously destroying (1) old culture, (2) old customs, (3) old habits, and (4) old ideas. Mao Zedong was convinced that because his revolutionary army of Red Guards were instructed not to touch the working class and agricultural communities, the economy of the nation would not be affected by the Revolution. He was wrong. The huge social upheaval caused millions of deaths from violence, starvation, and exposure. The self-inflicted poverty of Mao Zedong was plaguing the whole nation.

Esther was the third child of four, with an older brother and sister and one younger brother. She came from a long line of Christians. Her grandfather had grown up in the Soviet Union and immigrated to China right before the Chinese Communist Revolution. He had managed to leave the USSR before ethnic

Koreans like himself were put on trains and sent across Siberia to be forcefully relocated to Central Asian countries like Kazakhstan, Kyrgyzstan, and Uzbekistan. Although his Soviet medical education was a valuable asset to the community in rural China, he and his entire family were often singled out for persecution due to their Christian faith and the rampant hatred for educated people in those days.

Her grandfather and his family also suffered for their ethnicity. Chinese children were not very kind to ethnic Korean children and would often call them derogatory names and throw stones at them. Among his Korean peers, Esther's father completed the most schooling—but even he only lasted to the end of elementary school because of the intense and cruel bullying he and all Koreans endured there day after day. The most valuable education he received came not from school but from his father, who taught him rudimentary medicine.

Medicine became the family business, and, by the time he was an adult with three children of his own, Esther's father was the only doctor in their entire village. His job was not an easy one. He worked for almost no pay and had very few medical supplies. He actually had to work at another job by night, doing hard, laborious work, to keep his family fed. He had no support staff, no midwives, and no professionally trained orderlies to care for extremely ill patients.

Sanitation was so deplorable in the village clinic that it was actually possible for people to come to the clinic healthy and to leave sick. Small cuts got infected easily. Family members that accompanied their loved ones to the clinic could leave with an airborne disease from the germ-infested air inside. Without the right supplies, there was no way to disinfect the rooms, the examination tables, or even the medical equipment in a proper manner. There was no running water or electricity and the conditions were hazardous.

But there simply wasn't any funding available to change the situation. It would have been a crime to charge patients in order to replenish supplies, and although the village clinic was completely dependent upon the government, the government did not provide it with any funding. In those days, roughly 90 percent of childhood deaths in China were due to common diseases contracted from others. In 1967, the average life expectancy in China was only 57 years old.

Brought Back to Life

One day, the germs and bacteria that her father brought home with him from the clinic caused three-month-old Esther to suddenly became deathly ill. When her father realized that his little girl was seriously sick, he immediately began looking for a way to take her to a better hospital with more advanced facilities. He needed a car or an ambulance to rush her to the hospital, but no one in his village owned a car or even knew what an ambulance was. All he had was a bicycle. The hospital was miles away, but he knew his baby would die without proper treatment. So, seeing that he had no other options, he scooped her up in his arms, adjusted himself as well as he could on the bicycle, and took off.

He pedaled his bike as fast as he could down the rural dirt roads. Every minute counted but every mile seemed to be going by slower and slower. He was exhausted but did not stop pedaling. His survival instincts and love for his daughter kept him going. He pulled up on the handlebars in order to push the pedals down with even more force. Time was not on his side and he knew it. Whenever he started to slow down or even think about stopping, seeing the child's worsening condition was enough to keep the adrenaline pumping into his exhausted legs. He pedaled for hours until he finally arrived at the hospital. As soon as he arrived, he dropped his bike, pulled Esther up to his chest, and carried her through the hospital doors while yelling for assistance.

"My daughter! She needs immediate medical attention. Where is the doctor?"

The staff heard him yell and looked confused, but as soon as they noticed the little baby lying limp in his arms, they ran to assist him. Someone called for the doctor who rushed out to see what all the excitement was about.

Esther's father's adrenaline was giving him life even as he watched the life leaving his daughter's face. He quickly and carefully told the doctor about her condition. The doctor went into immediate action, yelling out directions to the nurses.

Frantically, the hospital staff began to work on stabilizing her vital signs, but her condition only worsened. Her stomach became inflated and wasn't releasing air. Soon she stopped breathing altogether. Her father watched in horror as her little three-month-old body became lifeless. He helplessly looked on as other medical staff worked hard to save his daughter's life. He wanted to help, to jump in the middle of it, but he knew that they were professionals. He also knew that he was exhausted, close to collapsing from exhaustion and dehydration, and could be no good to his daughter if he was unconscious.

He glanced around at the hospital as he tried to catch his breath. The hospital was not much better than his little rural clinic. The concrete block building was bare and not very well lit. The air was so damp, the corners of the room were black with mold.

Any other day at the hospital would have filled him with a bit of excitement. He would have been evaluating the tools and procedures used by the better-educated medical staff. Each room of the hospital contained objects and items that would have been nice to have at his rural clinic. After examining all of her vital signs and evaluating the situation, the head doctor finally realized that there was nothing they could do for the little girl. He focused his gaze on her to see if there was any improvement. He took her hand and held it for a minute to see if there was a pulse. He paused, shook his head, and then pulled back. After taking a moment to think things through, he gathered the nurses. After the brief meeting was over, one of the nurses walked over and pulled the IV out of the child's arm. Another nurse began to clean up the area to prepare for another patient. Her condition was hopeless. The father, who had been slumped in the corner of the room, suddenly stood erect.

"What? That's it? You aren't going to try to save my little girl?"

"She's dead. There is nothing else we can do for her," the nurse coldly replied.

"Move back! If you aren't going to fight for her, I will," he said.

Suddenly the large hospital and better-educated staff didn't seem so smart anymore. He methodically went through all of the life-saving steps that he could remember from his father. One by one, he exhausted each step by instinct. It was almost as if he could hear his father coaching him through it. He used every method he knew to try to bring his little baby back to life. The medical staff had never seen anyone come into their hospital and take over in this manner. They were half amazed and half annoyed. He threw his arms out as they approached the bed and kept them from removing Esther.

"If you aren't helping, get out of this room!" he demanded. The nurses retreated and watched the desperate father trying to save his baby girl. For a while, nothing seemed to work. Then, all of the sudden, she began to breathe again. To the amazement of everyone present, the little girl had miraculously come back to life!

God indeed had many plans for this child. This was the first of many miracles her family would witness in the years ahead.

Esther's life was extraordinary from the beginning, and it would be filled with many miracles that her family would witness in the years ahead as she bore much fruit for God's kingdom.

CHAPTER 2

Growing Up With Grandfather

Esther's grandfather, the family patriarch, was an active Christian witness in their community, and his love for the Lord would later have a significant influence on Esther's life. He preached the gospel even while practicing medicine in the village. Though his written copy of the Word had been taken from him and destroyed, it didn't stop him from proclaiming the Word inscribed on his heart. He just shared about the goodness and love of Jesus Christ from memory instead.

"Grandfather" had no personal possessions when he was sent by the government to live in a small village in northeast China that had no electricity, no schools, no clinics, and no running water. He was told to provide medical attention to the villagers, but wasn't given any equipment or funds to do so. How easy it would have been for him to throw up his hands and give up! Many people in China were committing suicide in those dark years; the passion for life was slowly being snuffed out of a whole country. However,

Grandfather had a larger vision. He did not live as if this life was all there was. He knew that God had not forgotten him, that there was life after death, and that although he didn't understand what was happening, he could trust his heavenly Father.

The love of the Father flowed from him in the form of a desire to help others. As soon as he arrived, Grandfather began building a well to supply the villagers with fresh water, a necessity for good health. If you were to visit that village today, you'd find that well still standing.

He not only loved people, but plants as well. He loved the idea of planting a seed in the ground and watching it grow. Plants need care and attention much like people and there were times that they would need extra care, but he knew that in the end plants would give back by providing food, beauty, and clean air. Grandfather planted many fruit trees throughout the village. If the villagers had a tree or plant that wouldn't grow, he would assist them until the plant was strong and healthy

He was also a handyman with a knack for fixing anything the villagers would bring to him. Everyone in the village called him something akin to "Jesus Freak," but it wasn't said in a hateful way. Many people said it endearingly. He had rare qualities such as talent, strength, intelligence, and humility that made him more necessary for the survival of the average villager than any of the Communist officials.

Grandfather was in love with Jesus and sold out for Him. He wore the title "Jesus Freak" like a badge of honor. It did not matter to him if people thought that he was crazy for following Jesus. What did matter to him was whether his family followed Jesus or not.

But as much as Grandfather enjoyed the title "Jesus Freak," the family hated it. No matter what they did, they could not run from it. They were inevitably guilty by association. Even though none of them believed in Jesus, they were still called "Jesus Freaks." Grandfather earned the title and the local villagers loved him. No one else in the family wanted the title, nor did they earn it, but the local people did not let them forget it. Instead of being a term of endearment, when it was used to describe the family "Jesus Freak" brought daily shame and humiliation. It was a weapon used by the villagers to keep everyone in Esther's family in line and single them out as different. Like a whip, the name was cracked out whenever needed. "Jesus Freak" kept them in bondage.

Esther hated the term even more than the rest of her family and whenever people used it against her, unexplainable anger rose up within her. She was confused by how Grandfather was admired like a king in their small village despite sometimes being treated like a slave. He was persecuted without mercy on numerous occasions, but somehow he always rose above it.

Those that persecuted him always found themselves in need of his assistance, so they'd knock on his door, often absolutely certain that he would treat them badly because of how they had treated him. They would be sure that he would refuse to help them when they were sick, or to aid them when their mechanical tools broke down and needed repair, or even to lend expertise when their little potted plants needed new life. However, it was not in his nature. He was committed to sharing the goodness of Jesus Christ with others. He often heaped "coals of fire" upon his enemies by showering them with help and love without even mentioning their trespasses against him.

His entire family watched this behavior in amazement. How could their family member, they wondered, allow himself to be treated like this? How could he allow the villagers to shun his wife and children and then turn around and help them whenever they were in need? Esther did not understand Grandfather's behavior and so became embittered at the idea of serving Jesus Christ. To her, Jesus allowed her family to be humiliated and then required them to turn around and smile as they served the needs of those who had humiliated them. It was like being humiliated a hundred times over. The ways of Jesus just didn't make sense to her or her family.

Because of all this, even as a child Esther firmly decided that she didn't want to be a Christian. She refused to acknowledge herself as such and tried to deny that her family had anything to do with Christ. She wanted to forget God and do away with any thoughts of living her life as a Christian.

Nevertheless, Grandfather never gave up on her and shared the gospel with her until his dying day. It would take many hardships and defeats, including physical pain, for Esther to finally submit herself to the Lord Jesus.

Sick Again

When Esther was eleven years old, she was playing outside with some friends when she suddenly felt intense pain in her stomach. Her father was away for work at the time in a remote location. As tough a child as they come, Esther avoided the sharp pain in her abdomen as long as she could, but eventually realized it wasn't dissipating and decided to go home to try to sleep it off.

Slowly and painfully, she made her way back to her room. When she got to her bedroom, she saw her sister standing by the bed. Hunched over, she walked past her sister without saying a word. Esther's sister watched as she moved in a peculiar manner across the room and crawled into the bed. Esther didn't tell anyone that she was feeling intense pain. Once in bed, she felt that she would be safe, but the pain kept getting worse. She pulled the blankets from the floor mat and wrapped them over her head. The pain kept intensifying and she started to whimper in agony. She grabbed a piece of cloth from the edge of her blanket and put it in her mouth so that she could bite down on it and keep herself from making noise because of the pain. She bit down as hard as she could and eventually became unconscious. At that point her sister realized that something was seriously wrong.

Her father had just come home and was getting ready to relax when he heard a scream coming from his daughters' room. He rushed into the room to find Esther curled up in the fetal position, passed out. However, she soon regained consciousness. Her dad stood over her and asked her where the pain was. Esther was unable to speak, but she pointed to her stomach. Her father recognized the symptoms and knew that she needed immediate medical attention. Esther's appendix had burst.

There was very little her father could do for her in the village clinic. He had no choice but, just as when she was a baby, rush her to the nearest hospital. However when they arrived, they found what looked like a ghost town. It was the weekend, and no one seemed to be at work.

"Hello?" her father called out. "We need assistance! Is anyone here?"

No one answered. There was not even a receptionist on duty. From the corner of his eye he saw a security guard approaching them. He ran to the guard and immediately urged him to call the hospital staff and get them to return to work.

The doctor on call and other staff arrived at the hospital a few minutes later. Esther's father ran up to them and began to brief them on the situation. The doctor on duty wanted to stop and take mental notes of everything that the father was saying, but as he paused for a moment, Esther's father grabbed his arm, led him to the room where Esther was lying, and continued to explain the situation to him. The staff followed closely behind listening to everything he said.

Once inside the room, the doctor made his own assessment and felt that it was necessary to begin operating immediately. There were several complications during the operation so the doctor diligently worked on Esther for hours while her anxious father waited outside, frequently asking for updates from the staff. After ten hours on the operating table, Esther seemed to be in even worse condition than when they had started. The doctor stood over her, exhausted and drained. The operation was finished, but as he took Esther's vital signs they continued to weaken. Then she unexpectedly took her last breath. The doctor was about to leave, but he paused for a moment and examined her again. There was no pulse. He glanced over at the nurse and with a nod they both understood what the other already knew. She was dead.

The doctor looked over at the door and saw her father peering into the room with a helpless expression on his face. He had been pacing back and forth waiting for any news from the doctor. He knew what it was like to be inside the operating room, but not to be outside, helpless. He was used to being the first to receive information, not the last. He certainly did not like the feeling of fear that grew with every minute of waiting.

The Prayer of a Righteous Man

Esther's grandfather had also come to the hospital. He saw the fear in his son's eyes and it hurt him. What hurt him the most was that the most powerful part of his life had not passed on to his children and his grandchildren. The God that he served did not reign in the heart of his son or his granddaughter, and as he stood in the hallway of the hospital, that knowledge magnified his pain.

He looked at his son and, with every fiber of his being, wished that they could share a moment of prayer. He wished that they could join hands together and cry out to the God who is in control of the whole universe. He knew that his family was bitter because of what they had endured, but he also understood that if the family would only know the love and mercy that is poured out from the Lord of all, they would never want for anything else.

Esther's father was so focused on the little figure lying on the operating table that he didn't notice Grandfather enter the room. Knowing that there was no one else who would join him, Grandfather began to pray. He pleaded with God to spare her life.

The doctor took one last look at Esther's lifeless body as her face turned the pale color of death. The doctor walked toward the door and slowly explained the situation to her father. The expression on his face went from worry to sorrow in a split second. Other family members who were also close by heard the news and howled in grief. A few of the family members stepped outside to allow the immediate family privacy.

Several of them even traveled back to the village with the news of Esther's death.

Grandfather continued to pray, believing with all his heart that Esther was meant for greater things and that her life could not end so suddenly. He fervently prayed for her to be restored to full health, as ridiculous as that may have sounded at the moment. He did not accept the doctor's report because he knew that the doctor was only able to report human observations and God was leading him beyond such limitations.

As he prayed, Esther's hand began to twitch; then her eyelids flickered a little. Not long after the doctor had pronounced her dead, the future missionary to North Korea began to breathe again.

"She is alive!" one of the nurses exclaimed in shock.

Everyone rushed to look at Esther. Could it be true? Could the doctor have misread the signs? Did the entire medical staff just pronounce the death of a little girl who was now breathing on her own without assistance?

The news swept through the hospital, but it did not reach her village until much later in the day. The news about Esther's death did not bring as much shock as the news of her coming back to life. The entire village knew her grandfather and knew that he was a believer in Jesus Christ. The rumors quickly circulated that Grandfather served a powerful God. Many people did not agree with him, but they no longer questioned or mocked him.

Esther's father and mother had just witnessed God's miraculous power. They had almost lost their daughter forever, but they had then seen God yank Esther out of the jaws of death. They rejoiced that God had healed their daughter and allowed her to live.

For a moment, Grandfather felt hope that his children and grandchildren might receive Jesus as their Lord and Savior. He wanted nothing more. He would have given his own life just to see his children join in the fellowship of Jesus Christ. He could not stand the thought of his family living for eternity in the anguish of hell.

However, the moment of renewed hope was short-lived. Esther's father was grateful for the prayers and the answer to them on behalf of his daughter, but he was not willing to believe. He stubbornly rejected the name of Jesus Christ. As a result, he was not able to fully discuss what had happened with anyone. The entire village had heard about the miraculous healing of Esther, but when people approached her father to ask for more details, he would immediately change the subject.

Even Esther herself did not acknowledge that God had healed her. She felt that she was too young to fully understand the miracle that had just taken place. Despite it being apparent to Grandfather that God had not abandoned them, the rest of the family still felt that God had left them to be unjustly persecuted.

The Legacy of a Patriarch

Though she didn't understand Grandfather's ways, Esther still loved him very much. As he got older he became feebler and eventually lost his ability to speak. Watching someone she loved, admired, and looked up to, grow older and weaker was very hard for Esther. She hated watching him age. She saw herself as grandpa's little girl and felt like he always knew the answer to every question and could fix any problem. It was devastating to her to see Grandfather relying on others for his smallest needs.

During the last months of his life, Grandfather was not able to talk to others, but could only communicate with his eyes and hands. It was difficult to communicate love and emotion in this way, but somehow he was able to relay sufficiently with his eyes. They were strong and had such depth that he was able to communicate emotions and feelings without saying a single word. His eyes communicated that he knew his time on this earth was coming to an end. He was on his way to meet his Savior, and he knew it. He would pound on his chest and point up to heaven. He spent hours looking up to the ceiling, knowing that beyond it was where he was headed. His days of suffering in China were coming to an end. He ran a good race and fought the good fight, and now his heavenly Father was calling him home.

One day he had trouble breathing. Again, he pounded his chest with his fist and looked up to heaven. Everyone knew that something was different this time. Immediately, Esther's mother went to fetch her husband and the doctor's bag.

Esther waited with Grandfather. She promised to stay at his side until her father came and as she sat there, she felt the anxiety of the moments passing by, each of which seemed longer than the last. Even though she had only been there for a short time, it felt like hours to her. Out of nowhere, she felt physically uncomfortable. She felt a short burst of pain in her head and at that very moment, her grandfather passed away. The pain left as suddenly as it had come. Grandfather had taken his last breath.

Esther sat with him as the color flowed from his face. His hand that she had been holding went limp and cold. The man who she had looked up to her entire life was now lifeless; his body only the shell of the strong-spirited doctor who had once seemed to hold the answers to every problem.

Grandfather did not leave earth without a trace. He had shared Jesus with many people throughout his lifetime, including with his family. He had also left the mark of "Jesus Freak" on his granddaughter. Everyone in the family was sad to see him go, but they also knew that they would continue to suffer because of his love for Jesus. Now the only person in the family who actually believed in Jesus was gone—but they were all still branded as Christians.

This was the one thing that Esther still could not understand about Grandfather. How could he love his family so much and yet allow them to be tormented for the name of Jesus? Couldn't he just deny Christ in public and believe in Him in private, keeping his faith a secret for the sake of his family? The logic did not make sense to her. He saw the pain that his beliefs caused everyone, but every time he was offered the opportunity, he still refused to deny the name of Jesus. To Esther, her grandfather had lived a great life and was almost a perfect man. His only flaw, in her opinion, was his stubborn belief in Jesus.

Though Esther did not understand it then, she would soon grow up to be a strong woman who mimicked the ways of her grandfather and his unwavering belief in the Lord.

CHAPTER 3

School Life

After Esther died and came back to life at age eleven, her parents realized that she was a treasure. They always encouraged her and reminded her of how special she was. Due to the special relationship between her and her parents, she often got away with not doing the same chores as the other siblings had to do.

It was also clear from an early age that Esther was academically gifted. She was well-known in her class for being an exceptional math student and had a dogged determination to do well at everything she put her mind to. She worked hard every day to excel at her studies in the way that her father and grandfather had taught her. Unlike in developed countries where children complain about having to go to school, in rural China school was a privilege. Not every child had the opportunity to attend primary school and Esther was going to take advantage of every minute of it.

Everyone at her school was ethnic Korean; the Han Chinese went to a different school. The Koreans and Han were segregated mainly due to geography. Although there were no Han Chinese at her school, their language, Mandarin Chinese, was still used as the primary mode of instruction because when Mao Zedong came to power in 1949, he made Mandarin the universal language for all of China. The Chinese society around her may have been convinced of the inferiority of the Korean race, but Esther was not. With a competitive heart and an insatiable drive for success, she approached every single day as if it were a competition, a race against everyone else.

Esther was known both in the family and at school for being strong-willed. However, she was also known for being generous. Even though her parents were very poor, they always encouraged her to have good manners and to look out for those who were less fortunate. This mind-set was not common at the time of the rise of Communism in China, but it was the residual idealism that came from Grandfather and his faithfulness to Jesus Christ. Even though the Communist government was able to turn the family against Grandfather, they could not keep his teachings from seeping into various areas of his family members' lives. Love and compassion are often contagious, even in godless countries.

The children at school all knew Esther's father because he was the village doctor. Because of the work that he had done, he had independently earned some goodwill among the villagers and their children which was sometimes passed on to Esther by association. She would also often bring extra rice to the school to share with those who did not have anything to eat for lunch. Esther's family did not have a lot, but they offered what they had to others.

Tomboy

Esther did not ever have new clothes and, unlike many of the other children, was not able to buy a school uniform. She always wore her older brothers' hand-me-down clothes, but they worked very well because she was rough on clothing anyway. And, being boys' clothes, they helped her fit in. She attended a small rural school with only about twenty students in her class, nineteen of whom were boys. Even though the teachers at her school treated Esther differently, most of the boys did not. They all treated her like one of them. Esther's brother was three years older, went to the same school, and would not allow anyone to mistreat his sister. Every boy at the school knew that if they did anything to hurt Esther, they would have to answer to her brother.

But it also meant that at recess, Esther had to play sports. If she didn't want to play with the boys, her only other option was to play by herself. But Esther didn't mind. She didn't like what little girls were usually interested in, anyway. Cooking, cleaning, sewing, and proper etiquette for girls in public did not interest her at all! Whenever she met other girls in her village or female friends of the family, Esther would try to engage them, but as she got older she gave up and hung out with the boys instead.

She would play soccer in the fields after school. She would run, play tag, and climb trees with her friends. If they had any extra money, she would go with a handful of boys to buy roasted meat from people grilling it on the street in small booths. Street kebabs were one of her favorite treats to eat with friends. Even though Esther was the only girl in her circle of friends, it didn't usually show. She could run just as fast and climb a tree just as well as any boy.

She didn't know it then, but this was all preparation for her future work in North Korea. North Koreans are known for being rougher and less sympathetic than their southern counterparts. This is not something innate, but is rather the result of harsh conditioning of living under the Communist system. Communism can be ruthless and heartless to the people under its control, throwing lives away like old rags. You have to be strong, tough, and resilient in order to survive. God in His sovereignty used even Esther's childhood experiences on the playground to prepare her for the task of taking the gospel to these rough North Koreans. North Korea is mainly agrarian, so the people are used to working with their hands and communicating in a physical way. As time has passed after the separation of North and South, the South has taken a more modern approach to development. South Korea has much fewer people who make a living by physical labor than the North. Esther's early exposure to rough-and-tumble childhood activities made her uniquely qualified for engaging and understanding the North Koreans.

Left Out—Again

All this does not mean that Esther was just a "country bumpkin." She was naturally blessed with the unique ability to understand complex concepts. Like her father and grandfather before her, she was intellectually curious as a child and did well in all of her classes in school. However, she was especially gifted at math. She loved the fact that every math problem had a certain undisputable answer that was absolute and made logical sense. A math problem began a small quest that Esther knew she could begin and ultimately arrive at a final destination that could be proven absolutely correct if she followed the rules.

Esther was able to grasp ideas and concepts faster than her peers, but she soon learned that there was a limit to what she could accomplish. She was stopped from progressing too far in her studies—and not because she was a girl. It was because she was from a Christian family. No matter how hard she tried, Esther was not recognized for her achievements. Every day she worked hard to gain the respect of her teachers, but was automatically rejected because her grandfather was a Christian and so, in the eyes of her teachers and classmates, she was a Christian, too. This label prevented her from receiving any praise or award that was presented to other students for hard work or achievement. As far as Esther's teachers were concerned, she might as well have worn a dunce cap with the word "fool" written on the front. She was an outcast.

Every year, the most excellent students were sent to the capital of their province to compete for their school—but even when she was ranked number one, Esther was ignored. Every year, she would watch the other students prepare to leave for the competition and long to be with them. She dreamed of what it would be like to have the honor of going to the big city to represent her small rural school. In some ways, it was like a badge of honor that she thought might even help people to forget her family's "shameful" past.

But after being overlooked several times, she found it difficult to continue competing. All of the goals of being a good student seemed to be completely worthless—nothing she could do pleased the teachers. No matter how hard she tried, they saw her as living under the black mark of Christianity—so she just gave up trying.

CHAPTER 4

A Chance for Change

Esther came home one day from school and pondered what to do with her life. She was grateful to have the opportunity to go to school, but that alone did not console her; she wanted more in life. She didn't want to just survive, she wanted to have the opportunity to excel. That was clearly not going to happen at her school or in her hometown, so she decided to drop out and to travel to the closest big city to look for work.

In 1986, when Esther was nineteen, there was a nationwide test used to discover the best academic talent in China. Esther's brother had already graduated from high school, but they took the test together. They both scored the highest in their region and the results provided her with a ticket out of the village. Soon she was given an opportunity to work at a medical testing facility in Shenyang.

Deng Xiao Ping was the new leader of China and he seemed to be taking the country in a different direction than Mao Zedong had. When Deng Xiao Ping came to power in 1980, he began to rebuild the economy after the economic disasters of Chairman

Mao by reaching out to the international community and forging ties with foreign nations. There was a feeling in Esther's province that the future would hold less suffering than the past thirty years, and Shenyang was starting to show signs of that progress.

Once she moved to Shenyang, Esther also felt more anonymous. Shenyang had a large population, and the people there came from all over Liaoning Province. It was a chance for her to have a new identity with people who knew nothing about her. It was a chance for her to start from scratch and build up her career through her own hard work and effort without having to be held back by her family's past.

Living in a strange new city had many challenges. Life was more expensive and you could not trust anyone that you did not know; everyone was a potential thief. Shenyang was a rough city back then and Esther learned that it would be safest to dress like a boy. She saw women being harassed almost every evening by men loitering in the streets, and she had no desire to put up with that. Esther was able to find some clothing that looked like what the local gangsters wore. During the day, it was clear that she was female, but when evening came, she blended in with all the guys.

One night while riding her bike home from work, a group of men stopped her and it was clear that their intentions were not good. Immediately Esther looked at the group and identified one of the more dominant personalities and began yelling in his face. All the young men were intimidated and stunned. They backed off, and Esther picked up her bike and continued on her way. She burst into laughter as soon as she knew that they were out of earshot.

A Persistent Grandmother

Esther felt full of confidence. However, there was one big problem with her new identity: her grandmother. When Esther made the move to Shenyang, she moved in with her grandmother, a devout Christian. Now, this lady was actually not technically her grandmother, but a distant relative who had offered her a place to live. However, Esther called her a grandmother because she was the same age as her grandparents.

Learning a new job in a new city brought a lot of pressure into her life. The hours were long and the training process was intense. When she left work all she wanted to do was rest. Her grandmother invited her to church several times, but every time Esther refused. "Esther, would you like to go to church with me?" she would ask. "Just one time, I really think you will like it." Each time her grandmother would ask that question, Esther grew less and less patient with her and after a couple of months would respond with yelling and aggression whenever the subject of church was brought up, eventually bringing her grandmother to tears.

Esther hadn't meant to be so harsh and abrasive toward this kind old woman, but excused it by saying that anything to do with Christianity caused nothing but terrible memories. Christianity brought out the worst in her. She felt badly, however, for taking it out on her grandmother, so one day she agreed to go to church with her in an attempt to make up for being so harsh.

The Christian church in Shenyang had been allowed to reopen in 1980 and restrictions on the church activity among local ethnic Koreans were starting to decrease. Her grandmother had been attending the church as soon as the doors opened.

Esther had never actually been to a church before. All of the churches had either been destroyed or closed before she was born and her only exposure to Christianity was through Grandfather. On the day she went to church for the first time, it was a bit intimidating and she didn't know what to expect. As she looked up at the church building, an odd feeling came over her. The ominous stone and brick building that towered over the street represented everything that she had been trying to reject. The church had been built long ago and had amazingly avoided destruction during the Cultural Revolution. There was a cross on the front of the building and it had a slanted A-frame roof instead of the traditional Chinese flat roof.

In her mind, the church stood for all that was illegal, rebellious, and non-conformist. It was the symbol of antirevolutionary teachings and behavior that conjured up feelings in her of hatred, rejection, and pain. All that she had promised herself to reject in life was bundled up in the symbol of this one place and yet she was willingly going to attend.

As she walked up to the doors, she took a deep breath and walked in. Once inside, all she could see was friendly faces that warmed the room with their smiles. They greeted Esther as if they knew her personally and it was apparent that they were all dear friends of her grandmother who knew all about Esther from her grandmother's sharing.

Esther was surprised to see foreigners there, too. China had expelled foreigners during the days of Chairman Mao, but on the day that Esther visited the church there were about ten foreigners of various nationalities in attendance. To even see a foreigner was unusual in those days, let alone to sit down and talk to one.

It seemed like in an instant all of the pain and animosity that had been pent up inside Esther for years finally began to subside. The power of love and peace was overwhelming in that old stone and brick building. Her pain from years of hurt and persecution seemed like a distant memory when compared to the love on display in that church. The people hugging her and giving her a warm welcome all had their own stories of loss and sorrow. They had experienced some of the same trials and persecution that she had—often even worse—but it seemed that they just did not carry the scars of past offenses with them.

The church was unfurnished and there were no seats or chairs inside the building. People just sat on the floor while listening to the old pastor who had survived the days of the revolution. Though there was a lot of love and joy in the fellowship, there was not a lot of teaching. Almost no one had a Bible or any type of teaching material because they had all been destroyed. Most of the people were too poor to purchase them even if they had been available.

Her grandmother instructed her to memorize the Lord's Prayer. Esther was suddenly eager to learn more about Christianity. She began to devour any Christian literature that was put in her hands. Knowing that Esther would rather read than eat, her grandmother looked far and wide and was finally able to find an old Korean Bible for her. The words in that Bible were written vertically like in the old days. Esther began to read as soon as she received it and was very excited to learn more. She would often fall asleep reading her Bible.

The Underground Church

One night, after she once again fell asleep while reading, God came to her in a dream and told her to visit another church. Esther didn't know that there was another church in Shenyang. She thought there was only one government-sanctioned church in the whole city, so she pushed the memory of the dream to the back of her mind. But she was soon to find that the next step in God's plan for her life was about to unfold.

One night, Esther attended a church meeting that was mainly made up of local university students. They came together once a week to study the Bible. One of the leaders had noticed Esther and her newfound dedication to serving God, so after the church service was over he approached her.

He secretly pulled her to the side and spoke in hushed tones. He glanced from side to side and was careful to make sure that no one else could hear him.

"You know, Esther, the teaching here is not that great," he said in a hushed voice. He looked at Esther, wanting to see if she understood.

Esther was a bit surprised. This was one of the leaders of the Bible study; how could he criticize his own study group? It made her feel a bit confused and uneasy.

"Esther, you put so much effort into these Bible studies. I really appreciate that," he continued. "After this meeting there is another meeting next week that I would like to invite you to, that is, if you are willing to go. I think that you would really benefit from it. The meeting here is," he paused for a minute to look around, "government-controlled."

Esther was confused. Weren't all church meetings government-controlled? All meetings of any sort in China, in fact, were government-controlled. China does not allow freedom of assembly. Until that day, Esther had thought that all Christians were the same. In her mind they all thought the same, believed the same, worshipped the same, and came together in any government-sanctioned church that would be the most convenient. When she realized that he was talking about an underground house church meeting, Esther stopped in her tracks.

China had just opened up and made it legal for Christians to meet, but instead of meeting at a legal church building sanctioned by the government, she was now considering attending a fellowship that was not authorized. If the police found out about this meeting, she would be arrested, lose her job, and ruin her entire life. This was not the way to build up her reputation! She had spent her whole childhood trying to escape the title of "Jesus Freak" because of the stubborn behavior of Grandfather. She had not only refused to follow in Grandfather's footsteps, but she had actively rebuked his entire lifestyle. For years she had been persecuted because their neighbors and friends thought following Jesus ran in the family's veins. Esther had made it her life's goal to prove them wrong.

Things had been going so well up to that point. She had previously stayed away from Christianity because of the pain and heartache it had caused her in the past. Was she really ready to willingly risk pain and heartache yet again?

The following week, the leader took her to an underground house church meeting. On that day and at that meeting, she knew she was proving everyone right who had persecuted her. She was proving that no matter how hard she fought against it, it was inevitable that she walk down the same path as Grandfather. Part of her wanted to turn and run. Part of her even wanted to report the meeting to the police, but another part of her—the strongest part—wanted to stay and worship. And so stay she did.

Esther never went back to an official church after that first house church experience. At it, she realized the wisdom of her grandfather and newfound grandmother. For the first time in her life, Esther let go of herself and fell into the arms of God. She cried out to Him. It seemed both foreign yet natural to her at the same time. God began to move in Shenyang and Esther watched the miraculous work of a true and living God unfold around her.

Unbeknownst to her at the time, God would one day use her to lead the same types of meetings in a place very different from what she was used to. What she experienced there provided the basic foundation for how she would one day hold similar underground worship meetings in North Korea. She would eventually see many North Koreans crying out to God for salvation in the same way she had cried out that very night.

CHAPTER 5

A New Life

The term "underground" can summon up images of believers secretly gathering deep in subterranean tunnels like the Roman catacombs or of candlelight services in deserted caves, but "underground" really just refers to the illegal nature of the house church meetings in China. These illegal underground churches are usually just small fellowships held privately in people's homes.

Esther did not know what to expect when she walked into the small apartment where the underground meeting was being held. She was timid and curious at the same time. The flat was just a small room with five other believers present, not at all like the official church. Yet as soon as she stepped inside, Esther could feel a sense of freedom even though the meeting was completely against the law.

The official church in China is monitored and watched diligently by the government, and its leaders are always on the lookout for any teachings that contradict the "China First" policy. Inside many official churches are large red banners draped across the walls that remind everyone to *Ai Guo* or "love country" more than God. In the small, intimate house church meeting, there was no such sense of being under constant surveillance, but rather a remarkable freedom expressed in the love and teaching shared between the members.

Freedom

The leader of the home group was not old like the pastor of the official church in Shenyang. He was young and very dedicated. His parents had both been killed during the Cultural Revolution. As soon as he began teaching from the Bible, his words immediately resonated with Esther. It was like listening to the words of Grandfather. The same spirit and the same teachings were coming out of this man's mouth as he taught the Word of God. His words were exciting and passionate with such depth and power that every one of them stirred her spirit. Esther found herself hanging on to every word, so much so that she was unaware of the amount of time that had passed while he was speaking. She was hungry to hear more. Her first visit to that small fellowship awakened a spiritual awareness in her that forced her to realize how hungry she really was for the Word.

The fellowship came together twice on that day, once in the morning and once in the evening, and still Esther was craving for more. Her mind was completely consumed with the desire to learn and to dive deeper into the Word of God.

As time went on, the home fellowship was eventually discovered by the authorities. The local police heard about the gathering and arrived unannounced. They told the leader that he was not allowed to have unauthorized meetings at his home and that the members had to attend the local church in Shenyang. Any other kinds of meetings were illegal and would lead to prosecution. From that day on, whenever the leader found out that the police were watching them, they would shut down the home fellowship and go to the mountainside to worship. This made Esther even more excited. She didn't care that the home fellowship had been closed down because she loved being outside in nature and praising God in the mountains. When they came together in the forest, they would bow down on their knees and sing out praises to God and it seemed as if the trees were joining them. The rustling of the leaves was like thunderous applause as they shouted "Amen."

Sometimes it would rain on them, but even that did not dampen their spirits. As they cried out to the heavens for the rain of revival, it was like their prayers were being heard. When they asked for their sins to be washed away, the rain would pour down from the sky and wash over their bodies. Nature had a way of heightening their senses and demonstrating the truths of the sermon.

One day on the mountainside, the members of the fellowship were praying together when the Spirit of the Lord fell upon them. Esther was caught up in the moment and praying out loud to God when she heard a strange sound coming from the others. Many of them were praying in an unknown language. It had never happened before and many of them did not know what was going on. The leader stopped praying and explained, "This is a gift from God; just let it flow. Don't try to stop it, understand it, or control it. Just let the Holy Spirit flow through you."

Esther stopped and listened to the others. She remembered hearing about praying in tongues, but had never experienced it before. Silently she listened to her brothers and sisters praying in a beautiful language that she could not understand.

"If you desire to speak in another language, just pray out to the Holy Spirit. All of us should desire to operate in the gifts of the Spirit."

"God, I also want to know You like that," Esther prayed. "I desire to have the gift of tongues. I have read about it in Your Word and want to experience You in a deeper way."

Silently she waited. Nothing happened. She closed her eyes tightly and waited upon the Lord, but still nothing happened. Esther continued to pray. There were people who were speaking in tongues who were new to the group. It didn't make sense; how could new members receive this gift from the Lord so quickly?

"Do You love me, God?" Esther asked. "Why can others experience You in this deep and meaningful way and yet You have chosen to leave me out? What have I done to earn Your rejection of me? What have I done that would prompt You to exclude me? Whatever it is, I will change it. I will abandon it. I will reject it if only I can know You more."

The leader could see that Esther was struggling.

"Esther, do not fret," he told her. "God is with us. We all have different gifts. Continue following after Him and seeking Him, not His gifts. The Holy Spirit is doing a good work in you. Do not let this discourage you. He is at work in your life."

Esther was not satisfied with the leader's words of comfort. She really wanted to receive the gifts of the Holy Spirit and to speak in tongues. After that prayer time on the mountain, Esther decided to fast and pray for a week to ask God to bless her with the gift of tongues.

A Dream and a Rejection

That evening she went home and started her fast. One day during the fast, she fell asleep after praying and began to dream. In her dream she was taken up into the clouds and as she floated up in the sky she was pulled to the northeastern part of China.

"Am I being taken back home from Shenyang?" she asked in her dream. "Where am I going?"

As she continued to travel in her dream, she was taken to an area that was clearly in the northeastern part of China. The clouds opened up and she saw far below her a group of people she didn't recognize. In the clearing of the clouds there was a beautiful illuminating cross and the sound of worship floated up to her ears. Time stood still. The power of the cross was overwhelming with its radiant power and beauty. The closer she got to the ground, the louder she could hear the people singing a hymn in a strong Korean dialect: it was "Amazing Grace." She had never heard that hymn sung with such passion and fervor before.

The power of the singing overwhelmed her senses. Esther could feel its power on her skin and inside her body. The voices came bursting forth, shouting praise to the power of the cross and giving honor to the sacrifice of the blood of Christ.

The dream was as real as life. She didn't want to leave, but it was obviously not up to her to decide. When she woke up the next day, she couldn't think of much else; the dream was such an emotional experience that it dominated her thoughts. She went to the leader of her underground church and shared the dream with him. "God has given you a gift, Esther. You might feel that He has rejected you, but He has definitely not done so. This dream has been given to encourage you to continue seeking Him. Keep your eyes on Him and never let go of the vision that He has given you." Esther was encouraged by the leader's words.

Brother's Conversion

At about the same time that Esther had left their hometown to go find work in Shenyang, her brother had left to be a police officer in Dandong, a town on the western border of North Korea where

Esther's older sister also lived. And while Esther was experiencing her vision, her brother was experiencing extreme stomach pain.

At that time, Dandong was still a small, undeveloped town without proper medical facilities. Esther's brother was in terrible pain and was hoping to find help in Shenyang. Their older sister had collected all of the extra money she could find and had handed it over to him. "Go to Shenyang, live with Esther, and get the treatment you need. They have good hospitals there," she had said.

He took all the money, added it to his own, left Dandong, and went to live with Esther for a few days. After arriving in Shenyang, he was still hesitant to go to the hospital. He wasn't sure what kind of pain he had, but was afraid that the money he had brought would not be enough to treat whatever it was. Even if it was enough, it was every penny he and his older sister had. He avoided going to the hospital for a couple of days, staying at Esther's home and anguishing over what to do.

"Brother," Esther said, "You really need to be treated for your stomach. You cannot continue like this. You are obviously in a lot of pain. It could be serious."

"I know," he said to her. "I was hoping that I would not have to go the hospital. I was just hoping that it might go away by itself, but it has gotten so bad that I don't have a choice. I just don't know if I have the money to afford treatment. I am worried that it will cost more than I have. I don't know what to do, Esther."

Esther paused for a moment. "Before you go to the hospital, come with me to a Christian meeting."

"Absolutely not!" he said. "Are you crazy? There is no way on earth you can possibly get me to go to one of those meetings. I am a police officer, Esther. What are you asking me to do? I can't possibly go and neither can you! Have you forgotten what our family has gone through because of Grandfather? Is your memory so short, Esther? Do I really have to remind you where we come from?"

He had more to say, but he was in too much pain to continue.

"I know, brother, I know every argument that you have against going, but Jesus is the one true God. Just like Grandfather told us, He has created you and me for a reason. He is the Giver of life and He can heal your body." She stopped there for a moment and then repeated, "I don't know much, brother, but I know that He can heal your body."

She looked at her brother. He was exhausted from the pain. He hung his head and buried his face in his hands. Esther put her hands on her brother's shoulder. "Come with me. You will not regret it, I promise." Her words sounded more confident than she really felt. She didn't know what would happen. For all she knew, they might go to the meeting, pray together, and end up getting arrested by the police. Then her brother would be in jail, sick, and without a job to repay any debt he might incur at the hospital. She stepped out in faith.

"Come with me brother. I know Jesus will heal you."

He really didn't have a choice. He knew that he did not have a lot of money and that Shenyang was more expensive than he had anticipated. He finally agreed to go with Esther to the prayer meeting and was prayed for by all the brothers and sisters at the fellowship. Soon after, he began to feel better.

After the first day, he didn't know if he was actually getting better or if his mind was playing tricks on him. On the second and third days he definitely did not have pain anymore. Esther kept a close eye on him and noticed that he was stronger and that his appetite had returned. On the fifth day it was clear that he did not have to go to the hospital at all. He no longer had any problems with his stomach—God had healed him!

He traveled back to Dandong to return to work. When he arrived there his sister was waiting for him, wanting to know what the doctor had said and what the operation had cost. When she learned that he didn't go to the hospital, she was furious. She felt that everyone had sacrificed so that he could take time off and go to the hospital in Shenyang. But when she learned of the healing that had taken place, her heart opened to the gospel and she received Jesus as her Savior.

It was not long before Esther's sister's home was crowded with other families who had come to the Lord. Though Esther's sister and brother were initially reluctant to take such a risk, they soon had more than ten families coming to their home for fellowship. Esther sent Bibles down to them in support of their effort.

The local police department heard about the fellowship and their meetings were raided. Her brother, a policeman, and her sister, a school teacher, both lost their jobs as a result of being a part of an illegal Christian fellowship. History seemed to be repeating itself in her family.

After they found out that they had lost their jobs because of the raid, Esther's sister and brother walked outside one night and looked up at the moon. There, in the dark, they saw a red cross on the moon and believed it was a sign from God that they had made the right decision.

Their choice might have been the right one, but it was not an easy one. Neither Esther's brother nor sister now had jobs to feed their families. Their father blamed Esther and quickly became enraged and bitter.

Esther's brother was making money any way he could. He began buying ginseng, storing it, and selling it again at a higher price. One day, however, he delivered a large shipment of ginseng only to have the receiver take off without paying the bill. The supplier then took everything he owned as payment for the lost shipment. He lost his house and all of his belongings and they ended up moving into a mud hut. Things continued to go from bad to worse and all the blame seemed to rest on Esther's shoulders.

Their mother would try to provide food for Esther's brother, sister, and both of their families, but their father was reluctant to help. He felt that they had lost their jobs out of foolishness, and now they must bear the consequences. He went off in violent tirades about how Esther was bringing back to their family the pain of the past. Her brother and sister traveled to Shenyang and cried out to her.

"Why did this happen to us? We tried to follow after God and He abandoned us when we needed Him. Look at us, we were doing so much better before and now we can't even feed our families."

Esther was devastated.

CHAPTER 6

Exodus

Esther faced challenges from believers in Shenyang as well as her own family. The more people she led to the Lord, the more responsible she felt for their spiritual wellbeing. The sacrifice required of those who came to the Lord during those days was great. Seeing the joy that came from a new believer being united with their Savior was powerful, but watching everything else in their lives fall apart as they endured persecution for the gospel was almost unbearable for Esther, and she felt personally responsible for their losses.

In fact, watching those new Christians lose their jobs and homes, just like her brother and sister had, filled her with unrelenting shame. She knew what it was like to be on the receiving end of that persecution and how it had made her so angry at Grandfather. Esther began to look for a way out. She wanted to escape from everything that was happening in Shenyang because it was just too much for her to bear.

Saipan

Wanting to run, her ears picked up on the news that many Chinese from her region were moving to Saipan for work. The little island of Saipan was unique because although owned by the United States, it did not have to abide by American labor laws. This combination created a very unique opportunity for American businesses to operate sweat shops in Saipan that mirrored those in China, even employing Chinese workers, while still being able to legitimately label their products as "Made in USA." This created the double benefit of getting American consumers to think they were supporting American workers while using cheap Chinese labor to maximize profits.*

There was only one exam that Chinese workers could take in order to be qualified to work in Saipan. If they could score high on that exam, then they would be considered for the chance to travel to the small island and work. Esther took the test three times and failed each time. However, for reasons still completely unknown, she was selected to go to Saipan anyway. Out of the two hundred people who had taken the test with her, only twenty-three were selected, and out of that group only a single plane ticket was issued, and it was given to her. No one else was provided a plane ticket to fly to Saipan for work.

For Esther, this seemed like an answer to prayer. She thought she would just go to Saipan and escape all her problems. Soon after taking the test, she found herself boarding a train to Shanghai, a city neither she nor anyone she knew had ever been to before. Everything seemed like a dream. She felt that she was being whisked away from all of the worries of the world to a new exotic place full of adventure and opportunity.

---

* The last garment manufacturer closed in 2009.

She was going to work for a South Korean company that had set up a factory in Saipan. China was so poor that going to an island owned by America seemed like a dream come true. She didn't know what to pack and what to leave behind. It was also her first time flying in an airplane, and she was nervous.

During those days, no one was allowed to travel without a stamp from the government. Esther had her ticket but did not have that stamp. As the day of her departure approached, she became more and more excited about the idea of traveling, but still lacked the stamp she needed from the government. The morning of her departure came, and still she had not received her stamp. She became worried as she realized that it would not arrive in time and that she would have to miss her train to Shanghai and the flight from there to Saipan.

She cried out in despair. She went to her church leader's house and cried. Then she headed out into the snow trying to figure out what to do. It was negative thirty degrees Celsius outside and her tears froze to her face. Her hands and feet felt like they were about to fall off. It was now an hour before her train was to depart, and she still didn't know where to go. By God's providence, she happened to run into a girl who took her to the provincial office. The office stamped her document, and by a miracle Esther made it onto the train, with ticket and stamped document, just a few minutes before departure.

As Esther sat on the train, all of the stress and worry seemed to fall off her shoulders. There was much to see on the train from Shenyang to Shanghai, but she was completely exhausted and unable to enjoy the sights passing by her window. In fact, the whole journey by train and then by airplane passed by in what seemed to be just a few minutes, and it was not long before her plane was landing in Saipan.

Finding Her Footing

Saipan, the island which Japan had lost to the Americans in World War II, by this time had become a tourist destination because of its warm climate and sandy beaches. As Esther stepped off the plane onto the tarmac, she suddenly realized how different Saipan was from the bitterly cold winter she had left behind in Shenyang. The heat bounced off the black asphalt directly onto her face. She fully comprehended for the first time how far away she was from her home in China—and the reality that she would not see her family again for several years suddenly sunk in. She didn't know anyone here and had no idea whether this would work out. She was living on an island and didn't even know how to swim! Overwhelmed and exhausted, Esther began to tear up before she even left the airport.

Esther was quickly scheduled to work six days a week from nine in the morning to seven at night at the factory. She was given a time card to clock in and out with every day and also the option to work "overtime" if she wanted to. The hours were long and the work was as laborious as it was monotonous.

Esther's supervisors quickly recognized that she wasn't the most qualified person to work at the factory. They watched her struggling to try to sew. She had never used a sewing machine before and tried hard to learn, but after three days it was clear that she was actually doing more harm than good. They tried to put her on the assembly line to fold clothes, but she did not excel at that either. The boss called her into his office.

"What are you doing here?" he demanded. "You don't know how to sew, you can't fold clothes, you have never worked on an assembly line. What good are you to me?" Esther did not know how to answer.

"Can you speak English?"

"No," Esther said cautiously, hoping that the boss would not switch to English just to test her.

"No English. That is just great," he said sarcastically. "You are completely worthless to me."

Esther sat meekly.

"Here, take this," he said, giving her a card. "Study this—and I mean *study*—and come back tomorrow. We will test you on the information on that card to see if you are of any use to us at all."

The card had a series of shapes and colors that corresponded to codes. The next day Esther took a test on the material and did exceptionally well. She was actually gifted at deciphering the information on the card. Instead of being on the assembly line, she was put to work keeping logs and tracking production.

Church on the Island

Once she got the hang of her job, there was very little for her to do on the island except work, pray, and study the Word. Esther was thankful to have the time to pray and was eager to start attending church. She asked her new colleagues where the church was and they told her that it was on the other side of the island, but that they were not allowed to go because it would interfere with her work and the boss would not be happy with her.

Esther was confused. She had thought that America was a free country. Why would Americans keep Christians from going to church? If she was not able to go to church, her time in Saipan was going to be unbearable! She eventually learned why church was forbidden: the owner of the factory was Catholic, but the main manager was a Buddhist. Because the owner was rarely at the factory, the Buddhist manager was free to implement his rule that prohibited workers from going to church.

When Esther found out that the church was only an hour away by bus, she began to dream about going to the church on the other side of the island. Suddenly, the other side of the small island of Saipan seemed so much better than where she was. Esther knew that it was against her boss's demands, but she reasoned that if she was willing to risk imprisonment by breaking the religious laws in China, she should definitely be willing to risk getting fired by breaking the rules at her new job.

As she watched and learned from the lifestyle of the workers around her, Esther realized that there were really only two things for her to do on Sunday. The first option was to work overtime. Everyone on the island was only there for one reason: to make money. The more hours you worked, the more money you could make, so Sundays were a great opportunity to make extra money without adding hours to days that were already excruciatingly long.

The second thing that people liked to do on Sundays was party. Alcohol was available to those who wanted it, and many people would drink on Sunday and spend the entire day intoxicated. The men would be roaming around the residential quarters looking for girls and many of the girls were more than happy to be found.

That was one reason among many that Esther was not really able to connect with any of the women. Although they were all Korean or Korean-Chinese and they shared the same language and culture, she just didn't have anything else in common with them. Most wanted to talk about hair, clothing, or—most of all—marriage. Many of the women who had moved to Saipan for work were lonely and desired a family of their own. In addition to making money to send back home to Korea or China, they wanted to bring a potential husband back to their mother and father. Still a tomboy at heart, Esther knew that she would not be able to spend every Sunday in the dormitories listening to another story about hair or prospective male suitors. She decided to find a way to get on the bus that would take her to church.

The following Sunday, she went out and waited for the bus, hoping that her boss would not see her. When the bus came, she quickly jumped on and peered out the window from her seat to see if anyone was watching. Through the bus window, Esther was able to get a real feel for the island. Saipan was exceptionally beautiful: lush and green with a backdrop of mountains and ocean. There were bright colorful flowers that she had never seen before. It was warm all the time with virtually empty tropical beaches. It could not be more different from northeastern China.

When she arrived at the church, she immediately felt the welcoming comfort of the Spirit of God. She walked into the building and, trying not to draw attention to herself, sat near the back and didn't really engage anyone. She didn't stop to take notice of other people around her or even listen to the sermon. To worship with others in God's presence was overwhelming enough and she spent the entire service sobbing to herself.

When the service ended, Esther was still not able to regain her composure and continued to sob. Saipan was different from any place she had ever known before, and she didn't have any friends there. She had never been away from her family before. The food, people, environment, and everything else made her feel disoriented, alone, and abandoned—but to be around believers brought the measure of stability that she desperately needed.

Training Ground

When she returned to the dormitories at the factory early that afternoon, the mood had already changed. Most of the people who didn't work overtime were drunk and empty liquor bottles were strewn everywhere. The stench of alcohol lingered in the air and was almost intoxicating to breathe in. Esther's heart broke for her coworkers. She could see that there was so much pain and hurt that they were trying to wash away with alcohol.

Knowing that, every time she returned from church, she tried to talk with her coworkers about what she had learned, but they just weren't interested. She shared the gospel with her coworkers every opportunity that she got, but she was rejected time and time again.

"I didn't come here to find religion," they would often say. "I came here to make money." Such was the life in Saipan. Despite economic advancement, life in China was still difficult for all citizens and especially for single women. Most of the money that these women made in Saipan would go to help mothers and fathers, grandmothers and grandfathers, or siblings' families that had children. Saipan presented an amazing opportunity to make money, but it didn't offer long-term security.

Though she was continually rejected by the coworkers she invited to church, she just clung closer to Christ and spent more time in prayer than ever before, praying several hours every day. She prayed for her family and church back in China. She prayed for her boss and also for God to provide a husband for her.

There was a man from South Korea who proposed to her, but Esther turned him down. "I am not going to get married," she would tell those around her. "I am just going to serve God my entire life. I am married to God."

She tried to say it with confidence, but the reality of her words never really clicked in her heart. Despite what she said, inside she longed to find someone to share her life with. She was hoping that God would find someone for her and present him in a way that would be immediately clear; Esther did not want to date or be courted. It was not a part of her culture or her desire to have a drawn-out relationship before marriage.

Several people at the church wanted to introduce her to one nice Christian boy or another, but none of their suggestions ever seemed to be right. She kept her eyes on Christ, but her heart was secretly longing for a young man whom God would provide.

Esther's prayer life in Saipan increased her boldness and she found herself in many situations where she was able to share the gospel with her coworkers. Esther felt that if she could not convince the workers to accompany her to church, then she would bring church to them. After church, she would return to the dorms and preach the same message that she had heard the pastor share. At first it seemed strange, but after some time the coworkers listened. Not only did they listen, but many of them started to look forward to the time of sharing.

Eventually, she started a small fellowship in the factory. Such experiences taught her how to preach and bathe everything in prayer, skills that would later be vital to her ministry in North Korea.

Esther shared the gospel openly, but was always careful to make sure that the boss was nowhere to be found. One Sunday as Esther waited on the bus for church, however, the driver made the mistake of pulling up to the front of the factory. Normally, the bus never came into the main yard of the factory, but always stopped outside. And, of course, just as the bus drove into the main docking area to pick up Esther, her boss happened to walk out of the factory building. Esther quickly jumped onboard and ducked to the floor of the bus.

Others passengers were looking at her like she was a crazy woman, but Esther knew that if the boss saw her, she would be in a lot of trouble. She crawled into the seat and laid low, then peeked up over the ledge of the window to see if he had noticed her. To her dismay, he was waving his hand to stop the bus.

Esther ducked her head again and started praying that she would not be seen. Another passenger recognized immediately what was happening, and quickly stood up to get the attention of Esther's boss as he boarded.

"Is Esther on that bus? I want her to come off right now," he demanded.

"No one on this bus knows you—you old fool," the woman shouted back in Esther's defense. Her boldness stopped the boss in his tracks. He didn't know what else to say.

"Well, what are you waiting for? Go on," she said to the bus driver. "We have a church service to get to." Without even thinking, the bus driver obeyed her command, closed the door on the boss, and drove away. The woman looked over at Esther and smiled as she sat down.

Esther consistently prayed for her boss. He was a particularly evil man and wanted to punish Esther for her belief in Jesus Christ. "Please bless him, Jesus," she prayed. "He doesn't know Your heart. Don't hold him responsible for his actions. He doesn't even know the evil that he is doing. Allow me to continue to show him Your love and mercy. May my life be a living sacrifice to You for him."

One day, the boss made an announcement over the intercom system while everyone was working. It was unusual for him to make announcements, so whole building paused their work to listen.

"Esther. Esther Chang. Come to my office immediately."

All the heads swiveled to stare at Esther. No one knew what she had done, but they knew that it could not be good. It was never a good thing to have your name announced over the intercom. She slowly turned to the office and began the walk of shame.

"Dear heavenly Father," she began to pray. "Allow me to react in a graceful way that will give You glory. Don't allow me to act in my own power."

As she opened the door, a group of men arrived at the office right after her. They were officials from America who had come to inspect the factory. The boss looked up at Esther, saw the officials behind her, and waved her off. She was never called back again.

Soon after the inspection, the boss moved back to South Korea. His departure was a bittersweet moment for Esther. She had always hated her enemies with a passion until the day she became a Christian and learned from the Bible that Christians are commanded to love their enemies. Since then, she had not really found anyone whom she would have enjoyed despising more than her boss. But her daily prayers about the situation had taught her many things about love and forgiveness, and had eventually swept away the bitterness. Now that the boss was gone, she was happy that she would not be harassed any longer, but sad that she didn't have any other real enemies to pray for. He had been her worst persecutor to date.

However, any lost opportunities were quickly forgotten when the new boss promised to arrange a free bus for everyone from the factory to attend church on Sundays if they wanted to. When the bus was provided for free, about forty people from the company began to attend church. Esther attended church services on both Wednesday and Sunday, and when a local training school offered seminary courses, she jumped at the opportunity to enroll. She also sent money back to her church in China on a regular basis so they could purchase Bibles for the congregants. After taking the correspondence seminary courses, the main school in America offered her an invitation to attend Bible school. She knew that she would first have to return to China to apply for a US visa. At that point she had been living in Saipan for three years. She knew it was time to go home.

CHAPTER 7

Homeward Bound

Before leaving Saipan, Esther bought all the Christian materials she could afford because most of the literature and media readily available in Saipan was still illegal in China. She purchased sermon cassette tapes, videocassettes of *The Jesus Film*, Christian books, and various other materials. After three years of living in Saipan, she packed up all her belongings and was prepared to board the plane back to China. As she looked out over the airport, thought about her coworkers, and took one last look at the island, she realized that Saipan had been like a spiritual boot camp for her. She had left her comfortable environment at home and everyone she had ever known, and it forced her to lean on God. Her prayer life had developed more than she could have ever imagined and participating in the amazing teaching at the church on a regular basis gave her the daily bread she needed to increase in knowledge and understanding of God's Word.

But while she was on the flight back to China, anxiety started setting in all around her. She knew that her luggage contained more illegal Christian material than clothing or anything else. And she was going to have to get it all past Chinese airport security.

Esther began to imagine what they would do to her at the security checkpoint once they discovered how much illegal Christian materials she was carrying. Her stomach started to hurt. If customs officials searched her and only found a single Bible or a few other materials for personal use, they might just confiscate the contraband and let her off with a warning, but if they recognized the *piles* of materials she was bringing into China, her criminal offense charge would be severe.

Chinese law had no tolerance for the smuggling of Christian materials, which they deemed to be counterrevolutionary propaganda from the West. China had spent most of the 1960s burning every Christian book, Bible, and teaching material they could find. Back then, the local authorities would hold large street protests where labor unions and student movements would force Christians to stand in the town square wearing dunce caps and signs with anti-Christian epithets around their necks while all their belongings—not just their Christian books—were burned in a large bonfire. Esther knew that China was still not friendly to Christianity and would not be friendly to her if they knew what she was bringing into the country.

She got off the plane, made it through the immigration checkpoint, and could see the customs officials checking bags as she waited in the baggage claim area. While she watched nervously, the customs officials stopped a man in front of her who had been on her flight from Saipan. The officers knew that the flight was full of workers coming from America with lots of money and items they were not able to purchase in China. It was their opportunity to not only stop illegal goods from entering China's borders, but also to take advantage of the workers by confiscating expensive goods or extracting bribes.

The officials found a cassette tape in the man's bag. He was reprimanded and forced to pay a fine on the spot. Esther's bags rolled down the chute and she could see that the customs agents had their eyes on them. Esther did not know what to do, so she just cried out to God for help.

Suddenly, her legs gave out from under her and she collapsed to the ground in front of the customs officers who all rushed to help her.

"Easy, easy…" the guard said as he helped stabilize her. "Are you okay?"

"Yes," Esther replied with a weak voice, still consumed with anxiety.

The guard took Esther's arm and put it around his neck as he helped her up.

"Do you have someone waiting for you who can help with your luggage?"

"Yes," she said as she pointed toward the exit. "My brother is here to pick me up."

Her brother was standing just outside the door and identified himself with a quick wave. The guard motioned for him to come through security to help Esther, and just like that, they were able to carry all those Christian materials past the customs officers without any problem.

At the next home church meeting, the members were ecstatic as book after book and tape after tape came out of her bag. During that time in China no one had access to such materials, so they were truly precious. This was the first time any such delivery had taken place at her church. They immediately began making copies of everything Esther had brought and distributing those copies to other local believers.

Esther's bags had contained more than a hundred sermon tapes, one of which became quite popular in the local churches. It was a recording of sermons from a preacher who had suffered greatly during the Japanese occupation of Korea. Since many Korean-Chinese had suffered similarly under the Japanese, his testimony was well-loved in the churches throughout northeastern China.

"Are You a Christian?"

Esther was a bit of an anomaly at her church because she was the only member who had been to another country. This, as well as her strong faith, made her quite the catch for the men in her area and soon after her return, suitors started lining up to ask for her hand in marriage.

One young man flew to China from South Korea just to meet her at the behest of some friends at her church. When he arrived in China, her friends came to pick her up, but Esther started feeling ill in the car and needed to return home. The young man eventually flew back to South Korea without ever getting to meet her.

There was one fellow in her circle of friends who had been working on a fishing boat in Saipan. He was single and looking for a wife. Esther was intrigued by the fact that he had worked in Saipan, too. She wondered if he had also thought it to be a spiritual boot camp. When they first met, Esther did not think there was necessarily anything physically impressive about him, but that did not matter to her anyway.

She inspected him up and down, then asked matter-of-factly, "Are you a Christian?"

"Yes," he replied without hesitation.

"Okay, then let's get married."

Esther did not believe in beating around the bush and had no interest in a long courtship before marriage. She would rather just let God lead her and submit to His will than work things out in her own wisdom.

Esther's parents did not really like Esther's sister's husband, so they were keen to meet this new fiancé, hoping he would be a better son-in-law. They were impressed by him and took to him immediately, so they gave their blessing on the marriage. Esther and her husband-to-be met in October and married in November. They were the very first couple in their area to get married in a church, although they also had a traditional, colorful Korean wedding held in the courtyard of Esther's house.

Esther had been praying for a long time for a good husband, but after only a short time of marriage, she began to fear that she had married the wrong person. He professed to be a Christian, but was not very dedicated to the faith. Deep down inside she had been praying to marry someone who had the heart of a pastor, but her husband was not hungry to serve the Lord at all. For him it was enough that he asked Jesus to live in his heart and that he attended church from time to time. Esther was frustrated at his lack of zeal.

Loss of a Grandmother

Soon after the wedding, Esther received word that her actual grandmother, the wife of Esther's beloved Christian grandfather, was sick. She rushed to be by her side. This old woman had harbored bitterness for years and years because her family was turning to the same religion that, she believed, had robbed her of her husband, her joy, and her freedom for all those years, but now she was quickly getting too weak to hold on to that bitterness. She was very ill, and the doctor said she only had three days to live. The hospital staff tried to give her an IV, but they could not find a place for the needle.

Esther went into the room and cleaned her up in preparation for her death. She tenderly clipped her fingernails, washed her body, and brushed her hair, all the while sharing with her grandmother about Christ.

"I had a dream a couple of nights ago," the grandmother shared with Esther. "I dreamed that I died and after I died, my spirit left my body and there was a woman in white clothes waiting for me. The woman's clothing was not just white, but brilliantly white, and they glowed with purity and cleanliness. The woman led me up to heaven and before me I saw these amazingly huge, beautiful gates. Just as I approached the gates I realized that I was alone. As I got closer to the gates, they began closing. I felt panicky as I got closer and closer, and sure enough as I approached the gates it became clear that I would not make it in before they closed." Her voice began shaking with emotion. "I saw my entire life go before my eyes like a collection of pictures. All the things that I have done, all that I could or should have done, were shown before me."

Tears filled her eyes. "I have done so many things wrong in my life."

In that precious moment, Esther led her grandmother to repentance of her sins and a living relationship with Jesus Christ. Grandmother lived for another month before finally passing away. Esther was at peace knowing that her grandmother would now be reunited with her grandfather.

CHAPTER 8

A Jonah Move

In the late 1980s, the Soviet Union was on the verge of collapse and so North Korea was rapidly losing her primary source of oil, a commodity desperately needed to keep factory equipment running and the economy afloat. Up to that time, North Korea had done quite well in building up local farming and industry, so much so that Korean-Chinese had actually flocked into North Korea for food and medical aid during the dark days of Mao's Great Leap Forward. With the loss of foreign resources, however, the little nation rapidly went into decline. To make matters worse, mismanagement of the nation's remaining resources by an incompetent leader resulted in famine. China was rapidly becoming wealthier while North Korea was sinking deeper into poverty. Millions starved to death in the 1990s; in some areas so many died that every inch of the hillside was covered with graves. Refugees began to pour across the river into China from North Korea.

Meanwhile, the church in China was experiencing huge revivals and Esther was excited. There were more people coming to Christ than ever before and church leadership was becoming more and more centralized. Yet she was also reserved about it all. A part of her wanted to fully commit to serving in the church during that growth period, but another part of her wanted a normal life. She longed to have a family, children, a nice home, and a stable environment to raise her children in. She did not desire the life of intense sacrifice that was required in China's underground churches. Esther's husband had saved enough money from his time in Saipan to buy a house, so they began building a family and settling down. In 1995, Esther gave birth to a son and her life seemed to be going in the stable direction she had hoped for.

But the same time, she could not rid herself of the sense that God had called her specifically to minister to North Koreans. Yet the whole idea felt far too overwhelming for her. The number of North Korean refugees in the Chinese house churches was increasing rapidly.

The church leadership continued to encourage Esther to minister to them. The pastor of the church told her to listen to the calling of the Lord. Even her husband pleaded with her: "Esther, God is calling you to preach to the North Koreans. They need you. I am just saying that maybe this is something you should take into consideration." That was too much for Esther.

"If I ever have to minister to North Koreans, then I will divorce you!" she shot back. "I cannot handle ministering to North Koreans and carrying a lukewarm Christian like you on my shoulders!"

Her words were sharp and intended to be hurtful. She felt cornered and wanted to fight back. She didn't like North Koreans and didn't want to have anything to do with them.

"Isn't it enough that I am serving You with all my heart in China?" she asked God. "Why do You have to add to my burden? Can't You find someone who actually loves these people? Why me?" Esther wrestled with God and tried to ignore His calling even though she could feel the Lord tugging at her heart every time she went to church and saw the North Korean refugees worshipping.

Back to the Island

Soon after her son's first birthday, she got a call from Saipan. It was the escape she was looking for—a company in Saipan called to offer her a job if she was willing to move back. Esther accepted the position immediately. She couldn't get out of China fast enough. She thought some time in Saipan was exactly what she needed. Esther gave her son over to her sister to care for and agreed to send her money in return.

As soon as she handed him over and waved goodbye, a sinking feeling came upon her. She realized that she was running away from God's calling. But she did not want to work with the North Koreans and certainly didn't want to go to North Korea. She wanted to be free from this inhibiting call on her life. In her mind, the best way to solve the problem was to get as far away as possible, and Saipan was the farthest place she could think of.

Though she was running away from North Koreans, she definitely did not want to run away from God. She just wanted God to change His mind about her calling. As she boarded the plane to Saipan, she befriended a Korean-Chinese girl who did not believe in Jesus. Her mother had sent her to Saipan with a special cloth to keep evil spirits away. Esther noticed it right away and shared with her about Jesus and told her that she would not need to use that cloth if she served Jesus. The girl seemed to be receptive to what Esther was saying but refused to loosen her grip on the cloth—in a place that was completely new, she wanted to keep this little part of home.

As soon as they arrived in Saipan, everyone was given a medical check-up and the young lady was diagnosed with tuberculosis.

After she found out about her condition, she sought out Esther and cried on her shoulder. "What can I do? They told me that I have to go back home because of my medical condition. Esther, I cannot return home. We don't have enough money for food. I need to make money for my family. Please pray for me."

"I can pray for you," Esther said, "but first you have to throw away that cloth because it is not keeping evil spirits away but attracting them. Only Jesus can heal you. You need to believe that. Are you willing to believe in Jesus Christ as your Lord and Savior? Are you willing to abandon all other gods? If so, God can heal you."

The young lady nodded her head.

"I am. I am willing to do anything."

Esther laid hands on her, began to pray, and she was healed immediately. They knew she was healed because when the young lady went in to take the medical exam for the second time, there was no sign of tuberculosis in her body. This miracle was one of many that Esther witnessed as she prayed for people and was indication that God was moving in a powerful way in Esther's life.

Life was different in Saipan than it was on her first stay. People from other Asian countries also came to work in Saipan and many were less willing to accept the harsh working conditions. The Filipinos specifically began to protest the conditions and a fight broke out. The protests and skirmishes got the attention of the American government, and new laws were put into effect to make things better for the workers. Esther was working at a new factory that gave her more free time, and she used it to begin a new correspondence course offered by a Presbyterian school in the area. Opportunities to learn about God abounded because many believers from South Korea had come to Saipan to minister to the Chinese. China was still relatively closed at the time and the

Korean Christians saw this as an opportunity to share the gospel with the otherwise inaccessible Chinese.

Esther took every opportunity to study, work, and serve at the church so that she would not have time to think about the life she had left behind in China. Although she could see that God was using her and was with her, He would not let her forget about His calling on her life to North Korea, not to mention her calling to be a responsible wife and mother.

Wrestling with God

Every morning she would go and pray for about two hours. Again and again God spoke to her about the place that she was running away from and the family she had abandoned. "I don't understand why You keep chasing me, God," she prayed. "Don't You understand that You have the wrong person? Don't You see that I am not well-suited for this calling? Why are You doing this to me? I miss my family. I miss my boy. I want so badly to be together with them, but instead I am here, running away. What else do You want from me?"

She cried out to God, but did not feel relieved. In her spirit she could hear the Lord gently directing her to pray for the people of North Korea—and so she began to pray faithfully for the people in that nation. She prayed for their government, for their laws, and for the country in general. She prayed that the gospel would reach them and deliver them from the nightmare they were living in.

One night she dreamed that she was once again taken up into the sky over China and was flying. She looked down and saw her son, but didn't stop. She kept flying. She flew into North Korea, and she could see soldiers in their uniforms guarding the border of that nation. As she flew past the guards she could see houses and was lowered down into one of the villages and landed at the front door of one of the homes. Suddenly the front door of the home opened and she was pulled in. She began to preach the gospel of Jesus Christ to everyone in the home, but it was not like the other times when she preached. In the dream she had no control over the words coming out of her mouth. They were just flowing in the power of the Holy Spirit. Everyone in the room was being fed through every word. Then suddenly, from somewhere behind her, came a group of soldiers with dogs that started to run toward her. She was scared that they would catch her but was not able to stop preaching. Without warning, she was then lifted up and delivered from the hands of the soldiers and their dogs.

When she woke up from the dream, she knew that it was time to go back to China and rushed outside to a phone booth. Looking at the phone booths had always only reminded her of the family she had abandoned. She used them to call home on a regular basis, and listening to her son chatting over the line was always heart-wrenching. Now, she could step inside and call home with the good news that she was coming back. She put in her notice at the factory, and on that day in 1999, returned to China.

A new life of self-sacrificing ministry awaited her.

CHAPTER 9

Ministry Begins

When she arrived in China, something in Esther confirmed to her that she was in the right place, but the feeling was bittersweet. In one way her return meant that she was doing exactly what she knew she should be doing, but in another way she was all too aware of the fact that she should have done the right thing sooner. She felt like God had to waste all that time convincing her and waiting on her to come back to China when she could have just obeyed Him in the first place.

Even after she arrived, it was hard for her to look at the North Korean refugees who were hiding in China. She considered them to be dirty, rude, and dangerous, and knew that there would be absolutely no earthly benefit in helping them.

Esther's sister, after repeatedly coming in contact with them, had started to serve the North Korean refugees. She called Esther and asked her to come and join her in praying for North Korea. For a period of about two months Esther stayed in her sister's region, and they went into the mountains along the border to pray over North Korea. They also prayed together with the North Korean refugees. The more she was exposed to North Koreans, the more her heart grew for them, but she knew that ministering to them was not going to be an easy task.

After a couple of months of traveling back and forth to her sister's home, she decided that the best thing to do was to fast and pray. She fasted for about three days, but on the third day she passed out and hit her head. Blood poured out of her head and down her face. Lying on the ground, weakened by the lack of food, and with blood running down her face, she began to cry. She didn't cry from the pain but from the shame. The futility of running from God became crystal clear. In that moment she felt ashamed for running away from the calling of God and completely surrendered herself to God and His will.

All of the time she spent in Saipan was time stolen away from her son. She couldn't even comfort herself with her wages, because a few months earlier a friend in need had borrowed all of her savings—and never paid it back. Every penny was gone.

Esther had no plan, no money, and no resources. But on that floor, she gave up her life.

"Not my will, but Yours be done," she said in her final surrender. "Not my will but Yours alone." On the fifth day of prayer, she cleaned herself up and got on a bus. She went to her church, stood before the pastor, and said, "Here I am. I am ready."

In Need of the Gospel

The pastor put her to work right away. There were North Koreans coming into the church who were filthy and had not bathed in months. It was Esther's job to wash their bodies and hair. Many did not know how to properly bathe themselves, so she had to help them with everything. Even if they did know how, they were often so weak from malnutrition and disease that they did not have the strength to wash themselves.

In the year 2000, God sent Esther the very first refugee that she would personally care for. This young woman, on the brink of starvation, had risked her life to come to China but was caught by the human traffickers who worked along the border river. Traffickers usually just ferry people across the river for money, but when business is slow, they lie in wait to catch unsuspecting victims who come across without a guide and can be easily sold as slaves. This young lady crossed the river alone and was spotted by a trafficker who caught her and convinced her that he would turn her in to the authorities unless she did exactly what he told her to do.

The traffickers brought her to several local Chinese farmers to sell her off. In northeastern China, selling North Korean women as brides is big business. The one-child policy in China has led to sex selection of babies; many parents abort their child if it's a girl because only a son can be expected to take care of his parents in their old age—it is not easy to retire without a male child. As a result, there are far more men than women in China today. Chinese men who are poor and live in rural areas are much less likely to find a mate so they often resort to purchasing brides.

The young lady Esther was caring for had been taken from house to house like a piece of meat offered to the highest bidder. A Chinese farmer eventually bought her and physically and sexually abused her over and over again until she was finally able to escape. While on the run she met a group of Christians who offered to help her. Eventually, she was brought to Esther.

Esther cleaned up the young lady and taught her about Jesus. When Esther started singing "Amazing Grace," the young lady joined in and sang loudly.

"You know this song?" Esther asked in surprise.

"Yes, my mother taught it to me. My grandparents were Christians killed by the Japanese when they invaded Korea. My parents were also Christians and they were killed in a prison camp by order of Kim Jong Il," she said, looking down at her feet. "My mother used to sing that song to me."

Esther saw the pain that this young woman had gone through her entire life. She had never really had a chance at a better existence. Her grandparents were killed by foreign invaders, her parents by their own leaders, and now she was running for her life only to be sold like a piece of property. What hope did she have?

Her pain filled Esther with chagrin. Here she was, handing out clothes, money, and food to the church so they could help the North Koreans, but she was only doing it to escape God's more intimate call on her life: actually meeting with, loving, and ministering to North Koreans.

Sitting in the room with this young lady convicted Esther that there was more for her to do than merely donate stuff to these suffering people. They needed so much more. They needed the gospel lived out before their eyes. What God was asking Esther to give was not going to be as easy as a simple donation: these North Koreans needed the love that only Christ could supply and Esther was the one to demonstrate that love to them through her own life and ministry.

Esther's Honeymoon in Ministry

As Esther committed to this service, her joyful "honeymoon period" in North Korean ministry began. God blessed her ministry, and droves of refugees began to come to her house for shelter, leaving as born again Christians! Every bed in the house was filled every night, and still more refugees showed up at the door. They started putting them on mats on the floor all over the house.

Every minute of every day was filled with serving others. Refugees came and went at all hours, so there was never time to get enough sleep. Not only was this an around-the-clock ministry, but it also came entirely out of their own pockets. Esther and her family carried the full financial burden, and it was not easy for them to make ends meet. Esther's husband decided that it would be best for him to go to South Korea to look for work so that he could send money back to support the family.

It seemed like the only way to continue at the time, but after he was gone for several months, Esther realized that she needed him home more than she needed the money. Being a mother and full-time caregiver for needy North Koreans proved to be too much for her. Not just because accomplishing daily tasks was a challenge, but also because it was too dangerous for her to be alone. Her refugee ministry had begun with young women and girls whose hearts were ready for the gospel, and at first, the conversion rate among North Koreans under her care was almost 100 percent, but after a few months things changed as male refugees started showing up. The North Korean men had a tendency to be violent and demanding, and Esther found herself constantly being challenged by them. As more and more refugees flocked to her home, more and more of them turned out to be thieves and brutes, lacking any compassion or emotion whatsoever.

The local church leaders were aware of the challenges that Esther was experiencing and often came to pray for her, especially for her safety and physical strength. Esther summoned her husband home, explaining the difficulties, and when he returned from South Korea an atmosphere of peace and calm was restored to their home. He brought balance to the environment. They decided that the in-home ministry only worked if they served together as a family. Despite the challenges, they continued to serve the North Koreans with joyful hearts—and as a result, many gave their lives to Christ.

CHAPTER 10

First Trip to North Korea

There was one refugee with whom Esther formed an especially close bond. Esther had led to her to Christ and discipled her in her home, and now they were friends. In fact, the refugee also shared a surname with Esther—which made them feel like family. When it was time for her to return to North Korea, she told Esther she would register her as a family member with the North Korean government. North Koreans are able, and even encouraged, to register distant relatives from China and then secure visas for them to come and visit. These visits are very important to both the North Korean people and their government because they allow food and money to come across the border in the form of family gifts which are essential to the survival of many people inside the impoverished country. The guards are able to get bribes and kickbacks from the visiting family members when they cross the border, the families are provided with a source of necessities for survival, and the government receives praise for being lenient enough to allow the visits. Everyone benefits!

When their invitation letter arrived, Esther and her family prepared to make their first visit to North Korea. Esther was excited and scared at the same time. She really wanted to see where the refugees had come from and what their lives were like in North Korea. She thought it might help her to understand them better and be able to better communicate with them.

In March 2004, after passing through Chinese immigration, Esther's husband slowly drove their car across the bridge that's a no man's land between China and North Korea. The guards on the North Korean side waited for them to cross the bridge, and she could feel their eyes piercing through her. Esther had looked across the river into the North Korean countryside many times before, but she had never actually crossed over to the other side. It became clear to her that she was a long way from her home in Shenyang.

North Korean immigration procedures were nothing like at the airport in Saipan. All the official policies and procedures seemed to be from the 1950s or even earlier. The immigration officers appeared cold and lifeless, operating like machines that did not smile, converse, or express any emotion.

From their dirty immigration booth they peered over at Esther's family and processed their paperwork. They didn't know any other life. Every day they gazed across the river at China and could only imagine what was over there. None of their television, movies, or newspapers told them anything about the progress China was making. They didn't have a clue about the financial changes that were making China more prosperous by the day. Such knowledge was deliberately withheld from them by their government, lest they get the idea of suggesting economic reform in their own nation or questioning the godlike status of their rulers.

Esther found herself longing to shake them awake and to tell them the truth. But it might not have been possible for them to believe. After all, they had been programmed since birth to believe the lies told by their government. The North Korean authorities had not been successful in conquering the South or in building up their economy or even in feeding their own people, but they were certainly successful in controlling the flow of information and instilling fear into every single human being within their borders.

Going Back in Time

The customs officials were strict and would not allow Esther's family to bring their own car into the country, which posed a huge problem for them because several gifts they had brought were too heavy to carry across. The customs officials also did not allow anything into the country with Korean writing on it. Only Chinese, English, and Russian writing was allowed, so any food items with Korean writing on the packaging had to remain in the car.

The North Koreans did not want their people to know that such things existed outside their country because their government had convinced its citizens that there was no prosperity for Koreans outside of the North. The North Korean propaganda taught that everything good for its people existed because of Kim Il Sung and Kim Jong Il. The outside world, of course, proved otherwise so the regime had to work hard to keep such contrary evidence out.

They checked the rice bags with bayonets, ripping the bags open so rice spilled on the ground for their taking. They shamelessly pocketed candy from bags, not even trying to hide the fact that they were stealing things for themselves. As government workers, they considered it their right to take other people's belongings. Once they had taken all they wanted they demanded that Esther pay a fee for the "inspection."

After the lengthy customs and immigration process they were finally allowed to enter the country. Esther felt like she was dreaming. She remembered stories from her father and grandfather about what China had been like after the Revolution and the Great Leap Forward and wondered if it was the same as what she was witnessing in North Korea. Many people on the streets were not even wearing shoes, just cloth sacks tied around their feet. Esther and her family immediately stood out as foreigners because they were so much cleaner and their clothes were in much better shape than everyone else's. A local resident would have never been allowed to wear nice clothes like Esther and her family wore.

As she looked around, Esther suddenly realized she was pinching her own arms until they bruised because everything was so unreal—like a nightmare. Even her friends, the refugees who had lived in her home and who had provided her with the invitation letter, seemed reserved and distant when they met Esther at the border. She quickly realized that being back inside North Korea had a powerful effect on their psyches. The wretchedness all around opened Esther's eyes to why many of the refugees she helped were so dishonest and emotionless.

As they continued down the road they saw an older man who was about forty years old and a young child riding bikes in the same direction. The two bikes bumped into each other and the boy fell to the ground and seemed to be hurt badly. The old man stopped his bike, walked over to the boy, and, instead of helping him up, began to beat him! Esther's family looked on in horror as this man kept beating a little boy who had just had a bike accident.

It was not long before they arrived at their friend's home. The house was very poor and looked like the shoddy village homes that were in northeastern China during the Cultural Revolution. Many of them were made of wood with chimneys reaching out to the sky through broken, mismatched, wooden tile roofs. Each chimney represented a family or two and there were several chimneys per wooden structure.

The home was dark inside. Dust floated in the air but could only be seen in the brief moments when daylight broke through the window or a crack in the wood. Inside their home, pictures of Kim Jong Il and his father Kim Il Sung—the founder of North Korea—were prominently displayed on the wall. The pictures were the central attraction in their home and the nicest items they owned. All North Koreans are responsible for the upkeep of these household treasures. If the picture frame breaks, the glass gets dirty, or the picture is damaged in any way, the homeowners are subject to harsh punishment for insulting their leaders.

Other than the pictures, the house of this North Korean family was almost totally empty. There was nothing to do inside but to sit and look at each other. There were no video game consoles or board games to play. There weren't any local parks or tourist sites. Everything seemed to be covered in a dark cloud of depression.

A Pile of Rags on the Railroad

Her host family was very generous and shared what they had with her. Since she was considered family, she was given much freedom to view the area without the police escort required for most foreign visitors. The next day they all went out for a walk and saw a large shade tree on the side of the road with several people sitting in a circle under it. As Esther and her family got closer, they could see the people were holding a man who seemed weak and sick.

"What is wrong with him?" Esther asked.

No one responded. They were all slumped over and seemed lethargic. Again Esther asked, "Is there something wrong here?"

One person looked up with lifeless eyes at Esther and answered, "He is dead."

Esther stopped. She was shocked. No one was crying or show-ing any signs of grief. No police or ambulance had come to help this man or to take him away. It was not clear how long he had been dead, and no one else seemed to even notice the people under the tree.

As they walked on along the railroad tracks, Esther could see something in the distance that looked like a messy pile of clothes. When she got closer she saw that it was actually an emaciated young girl, lying there dead.

Esther had seen dead people before, but had never experienced this type of disregard for a body. No one seemed to care that this young girl had fallen down and died right there on the train tracks.

Esther looked at her face. It was lifeless, but not much dif-ferent from the faces of the North Koreans surrounding her who were still alive. She had died without hope and most likely without knowing Jesus as her Lord and Savior. The longer Esther looked at her face, the more she imagined her own face and body lying there.

At that moment Esther realized that there really was no dif-ference between that dead girl and herself. If she had been born on the other side of the border, she would have been the same—a cold, lifeless, emotionless, dishonest thief on the verge of starvation. The only difference between that young girl and her was which side of the border they were born on. Esther was overcome with guilt for her past feelings of judgment and pride. "Dear Lord," she cried out. "Forgive me! Forgive me for all of the sin I have committed. Forgive my disobedience. Forgive my stubbornness and lack of desire to follow Your will. Forgive me for all the times I denied Your name or disobeyed Your calling."

Esther begged God for forgiveness like she never had before. "If I had not run away maybe I would have had a chance to share the gospel with this girl. Maybe if I was not trying to do what I wanted and had followed Your will instead, she might still be alive.

"Dear God, there is nothing I can do about this now. I can't go back in time. I can't undo what I have done. I just wish I could turn back the hands of time so I could follow Your will from the beginning. I have failed You, Father, I have failed You!"

"One Born in Hell Naturally Acts Like a Devil"

But in that moment of repentance, God revealed to Esther a clear purpose and connection between her and the North Korean people. Now she understood why Grandfather was trained in Russia and persecuted in China. Now she knew why she was born, privileged, in China and lived the life she had lived. There was a clear connection between her life and everything God had told her to do. In the stillness of that moment, Esther felt God speak to her, saying, *I have called you. I have prepared you.*

Esther knew she had been called by name to devote her life to God's service to the North Korean people.

Before that day, there were times when Esther felt completely betrayed by the North Koreans she was trying to serve. She was putting her livelihood on the line for them, and they responded with cruelty, thievery, and verbal abuse. But now she realized that those without God know of no other way to act. One born in hell naturally acts like a devil.

"I will preach Your Word, Lord, even if it costs me my life. I will share as much as I can before they kill me. I want to see as many people saved as possible," she prayed passionately.

Esther went back to her friend's home emotionally and spiritually exhausted. Being in North Korea was proving to be a sensory overload for her. It felt like being in an alternate universe where life was backward: everything that was normally right was wrong, and all that was wrong was right.

Later that night, she saw a man on his way home to the next village over. He stood out from all of the other men in the village because of his handsome features. He looked like a movie star! She learned from her friends that the man's wife had just starved to death. Apparently, shortly after his wife's death, his young daughter had invited a friend over to play. The playmate then went missing.

The night that Esther saw him, local authorities were alerted to his home because of the missing girl, and they arrived to a scene of unimaginable horror. A large pot of water was sitting over the fire, boiling the body parts of the missing little girl.

Even more astounding, no one in the village seemed surprised at all. What shocked Esther and her family was simply shrugged off by these North Koreans.

That first trip to North Korea was one of Esther's most life-changing experiences. She was in a mild state of shock when she returned to her home in China, and it took her some time to digest everything she had witnessed. Nothing could have prepared her for the deprivation and the grisly pain. But none of the darkness of North Korea could dampen the love in Esther's heart for these lost souls. On the contrary, the more she saw, the more compassion she felt for the people and the more she longed to see them come to Christ.

After a few days of recovery, it was back to life as usual serving the refugees in her home. She had only been in North Korea one time, but she knew it would not be the last. God had called her to serve the North Koreans and she realized that her ministry may require her to cross the border again and again.

CHAPTER 11

Paying the Price

One day the phone rang.

"Are you Esther?" a rough voice asked when she picked up.

"Yes," she replied cautiously.

"We need you to give us 500 Chinese Yuan," the voice said abruptly.

"I am sorry, but I don't know you," Esther said in confusion.

"Get the money ready and we will send someone to pick it up. If you don't hand the money over to us we will track down your son and make him a cripple for the rest of his life!"

With that, the caller hung up.

Esther froze. She had never had a phone call like that in her life. She wondered what to do. If she called the police, they would find out that she was illegally hiding North Korean refugees in her home—and not only hiding, but also preaching the gospel message to them. Doubly illegal. She couldn't do anything but pray.

And keep working.

Esther prepared Bible studies and taught from the Word of God every day. Whenever new refugees arrived, she would serve them food and wash their lice-ridden hair. She cooked all their meals, made all their beds, and cleaned every room by herself. She slept on the floor with some of the refugees because she had given all the beds out to others. She soon began to receive phone calls from North Koreans just arriving in China who were asking, and sometimes demanding, aid. She was constantly on alert, moving and working, and she could feel herself burning out.

The day after the phone call, five needy North Koreans showed up at her door. She brought them in, tended to their needs, fed them, and got them situated and adjusted in their rooms. No sooner had she finished, another knock came at the door. When Esther answered it, there were another five North Koreans waiting at the door. Just as any other day, there was no time to rest. They were all so dirty that just having them in the house was dangerous for hygienic reasons. They all had lice in their hair and fungus growing on their skin. She needed to get them all to the public bathhouse as soon as possible before they spread lice and diseases in her home.

None of the women had bras or even underwear and all their clothes had a horrible odor. Esther walked away from them, went into the bathroom by herself, closed the door, and began crying. Everything just seemed so overwhelming. Including the threatening phone call.

"Dear Lord, help me," she prayed, "I need Your help."

Esther had been able to understand the refugees better after seeing the environment they had come from and how they had lived before knocking on her door. But even with her new understanding, the continuing situation was still difficult, dangerous, and proving to be almost unbearable.

She composed herself, walked back out, and took everyone to the public bathhouse to get them washed up. Before they walked into the bathhouse, Esther turned to them and said, "Nobody can speak a word. Do you understand me? You must remain completely silent. Don't speak to anyone. Your accents will give you away. If you speak, everyone will know you are from North Korea and we will all be arrested."

"Why do you do this for us?" they asked. "What are you getting out of this? Why do you risk so much to help us?" They were all in need of her help and had nowhere else to go, but they were also confused by her desire to help. Who would risk going to jail to help people they had never met and had no family obligations to?

"I do what I do because of the Lord Jesus Christ. He loved me before I knew Him and I in turn love others before they know me. It is what I have learned from following Him." It still did not make sense to them, but Esther did not have time to explain in more detail.

When they went back to the house, many of them received Jesus Christ as their Lord and Savior and Esther was able to share with them from the Scriptures. There were others, however, who secretly resented her. They were willing to accept all the help she could offer, but secretly plotted against her.

The Breaking Point

The next evening, Esther came home and saw a North Korean yelling at everyone in the house.

"What is wrong here?" Esther asked.

"You! You are the problem. I need money," he demanded.

"What are you doing? I am trying to help you, why are you doing this?"

"I don't need your help. I need all of your money."

At that very moment, Esther's six-year-old son came out of one of the bedrooms and the man grabbed him and pulled him into his arms. He grabbed a kitchen knife from the table and put it up to the child's neck. Esther screamed.

"Get back! Get back or I promise you I will slit his throat," he yelled.

Esther's son started crying for him to stop.

"Please. Don't hurt my son," Esther tried to say calmly.

"I told you. Give me your money. Give it all to me or I will fill this room with his blood. Do you hear me?"

"Okay, okay," Esther said, shaking uncontrollably as she dumped everything out of her handbag. "This is all the money that I have. Take it. Please don't hurt my son."

The man tossed her son to the side, grabbed the money, and walked out the door. Esther reached for her son and held him tightly. She cried into his chest as she held him there on the floor. But Esther's son pushed her away and slapped her face.

"Why do you love them more than me?" he demanded, pointing the other refugees in the house. "Why, mommy? Are *they* your sons? I am sick all the time because of their diseases. I can't go to school. When you are not here, they take my food. They don't even let me eat, mommy. They told me that if I told you they would hurt me. Why are you doing this to us?"

Esther was speechless. Everything he said was true. To hear her six-year old son speak like a grown man made her realize that his childhood was being stolen from him. He had lice and skin rashes because of the environment he was living in. His fingernails were worn down to the skin and dried blood was at every tip because he chewed them incessantly from nervousness. She hadn't known that he was being abused in her absence, but it was clear to her now.

Esther wept and opened her arms out to him. He ran into her arms, and they hugged and cried together, but the moment was short-lived. The phone rang again. It was her friend calling to tell her that some North Korean refugees had been caught by the authorities and, in desperation, had told them that Esther was abusing refugees in her home and using them for money. The police now knew exactly what she was up to.

Stunned, Esther was unable to process what this meant.

"Esther!" her friend said again. "You need to leave your house immediately. The police are looking for you."

Esther left the phone dangling off the hook. The whole world seemed to be crashing down around her. Her husband was away on a business trip, her son had been terrorized in her own home, she had just been robbed of all her money, and now she had to flee her home because the police were after her. She scooped her son up in her arms and started walking toward the door.

"Everyone here needs to leave!" she yelled. "The police are coming and they will arrest you if you are here."

"Where should we go?" one of the refugees whimpered.

Esther paused for a moment and then quickly responded, "I don't know," and left.

She walked out of house with her son, but didn't know where to go, either. She walked all the way to a former coworker's home who used to evangelize North Korean refugees. Esther thought that the evangelist might understand their situation, but instead of taking them in and helping them, he shut the door in their faces because he was afraid that Esther would bring the police to his house. In fact, he was angry at Esther for coming to his home and possibly putting his own family in danger. He had stopped ministering to North Koreans years ago out of this fear.

Esther roamed the streets with her small son. They were hungry and tired and had nowhere to sleep, nothing to eat, no money, and no one to call for help. All she could do was pray. At last, after walking all the way to the edge of town, she just sat down with her son beside a desolate road. "Everything will be okay," she said to her son as he cried. But inside she knew that she was just as scared as he was. She was afraid of what the next moments without food, shelter, or money would look like. She was vulnerable to the elements and had no one to rely on. Her son cried because of hunger and she tried to comfort him with what little strength she had left. Holding her son, crying and praying, she called out to God.

"God will take care of us. We only need to trust in God. He will aid us."

This would not be their first time on the streets with nothing. Esther would continue to be betrayed by the North Korean refugees. Some of them would eat until they were completely full and then turn around and tell others that they had been starving in China because of Esther. They would take everything she had and then do everything they could to get her in trouble once she ran out of resources.

Many of them acted like cold-blooded animals without hearts or souls. Esther knew that Jesus wanted her to love them, but their behavior was abnormal and beyond anything she was prepared to deal with. There was a part of her that wanted to receive at least a small amount of gratitude for what she had done for them. Yet not only were they thankless; they actually wanted to harm her for helping them. Nothing was like what she had expected.

The next day she heard that some of the North Koreans from her home had moved on to a local church and that the others had returned to North Korea. She decided to go back home. She didn't care if she got caught. She was just tired of running.

CHAPTER 12

Return to North Korea

Esther had often told herself that she may have lost everything else, but at least she had her health. Now even that was being taken away from her. A few days after being turned onto the street, she started to feel weak and kept vomiting. It was not long before she had to be taken to the local hospital. The stress of constantly being in danger had taken its toll: the doctor told her that she had stress-induced stomach inflammation, a heart murmur, and hardening of her arteries that was causing blood circulation problems. She was in critical condition and needed immediate treatment.

As she lay there helpless and exhausted, she oddly didn't feel fearful. She knew that God was teaching her through the whole painful process. Even as she recollected how she had been abused by the refugees, she was also reminded that Jesus loved all of His disciples and chose Judas even though He knew full well that Judas would betray Him. Judas even tried to profit from His suffering, but Jesus loved him anyway. He invested time, love, and energy into discipling Judas, trusting him with all their funds.

Jesus must not have considered any of it a waste, because the Son of God doesn't waste anything.

In the midst of such great weakness, all she could do was give everything up to God in prayer—her own health, the abusive refugees, her son, her husband, their church, everything. As she focused on entrusting her situation to the Lord, her condition improved rapidly and she felt God's healing hand upon her. The awestruck doctor had to admit that he could no longer find anything wrong with her. She walked out of the hospital much sooner than expected and immediately went to work packing up her home before the police returned.

After moving to a new house, she went back to the church and found new North Korean refugees already waiting there for her. God had restored her strength while she lay on that hospital bed and she proceeded to throw herself back into ministry.

Open Doors

God began to open doors for her to have unprecedented access to North Korea. Through a special connection, she was able to get a job as a consultant for a Chinese company doing business in North Korea. The company needed her to oversee many long-term projects which enabled Esther to stay in North Korea for as long as she wanted. Even the State Police Security Department (SPSD) officers were surprised by the lack of limitations on her visa. She packed her bags to enter the country.

A visitor to North Korea is usually assigned one or two guides who follow their assigned visitors everywhere, determine where they can go and who they can meet, and closely monitor everything, all at the visitors' expense. It turned out that no guides were available when Esther crossed the border this time, so she was amazingly allowed to continue on without one.

On the road to her destination, there were several check-points. Had she been a local resident, she would have had to show her ID card at every checkpoint. When the security guards saw her at each stop, they initially harassed her because they thought she was a North Korean with nice clothes, but when she showed her passport they immediately recognized that she was a Chinese citizen and left her alone.

This second trip was no less shocking to Esther than her first one had been. Again, she felt like she was going back in time. The people were dressed in soldier uniforms with old belts around their waists. Workers would march from place to place with red flags in their hands signifying revolution. Their old dusty uniforms hung loosely on their gaunt skeletal frames and their red armbands had to be pinned in place because their arms were too small in diameter to keep the armbands from falling down. Their shoes were also rotten and full of holes. Their faces were pale and had no signs of life or happiness in them.

This time she felt like she was able to see everything around her with two different sets of eyes: her physical eyes and her spiritual eyes. She could see that the land was clearly full of idolatry. Everywhere she looked, she could see that the people were worshiping the two leaders, Kim Jong Il and Kim Il Sung. The people were without joy and had no compassion for their fellow human beings. Everyone was in a constant state of starvation, and the land was clearly cursed because of its idolatry and hatred toward Christianity.

As she walked down the streets, she could see the poverty in every home. From the outside, the village houses didn't look particularly bad, but when you looked inside, the poverty was evident. They had dirt floors without any sort of rugs. The families inside had nothing to eat except for a little porridge made from grass and powdered corn or ground corncobs. This kind of porridge is not much different than low-grade cattle feed in other countries.

Those who could not afford even porridge at times became so hungry that some of them would kill their own relatives just to eat them for survival, as Esther had witnessed on her first trip. Everywhere she looked there was fighting, violence, and profanity. People were dying along the sides of the streets and their bodies were disregarded as if they were only garbage waiting to be picked up on the curb.

Esther wanted to lift up her hands and shout from the middle of the town square, "Believe in Jesus and be saved!" but knew that she would have been killed without question. She had to find a way to preach the gospel of Jesus Christ without the local authorities finding out.

As the North Korean government is involved in every aspect of its citizens' lives, it would not be easy for her to avoid detection. And yet, Esther could feel the Father's burden for North Korea and His desire to bring its people back to Him. The blood of many martyrs had been spilled on North Korean soil and she knew that sacrifice would one day reap great eternal rewards.

Food for the Hungry

After Esther had made a few more trips to North Korea, some Chinese businessmen contacted her. They were looking for opportunities to expand in the reclusive country and felt that Esther would be the best person to show them the ropes. Esther jumped at the chance and, by bringing in so many large investors, quickly became well-known among the border guards and North Korean officials.

The officials all eyed her with a bit of suspicion. No other foreigner came to live with the people for such long periods of time.

No one else was arranging truckloads of desperately needed supplies from China without any interest in turning a profit. She was truly an anomaly and that alone made her subject to distrust. However, she was well-liked by the government because she was the only one who could procure large shipments of goods from different companies. They viewed her as an amazing asset for the people of North Korea.

But she brought in much more than investors.

Along with all the other shipments of goods, she would also bring with her items to give away, items that she knew were desperately needed such as rice, sugar, and flour. She wanted to bring Bibles into the country, but had decided early on to only enter the country in a lawful manner.

Esther would often take a pig with her and cook it on her first or second night in North Korea. People would smell the sweet smell of pork cooking and come from miles around to knock on the door. They claimed that they would like to buy some of the food, but everyone in the house knew that they didn't have any money and were hoping to get some for free. It seemed like the whole population of North Korea was starving and just wanted a little meat in their diet.

No matter who came to the door, Esther would make sure that they received something. She would hand out pork, rice, soup, and whatever she could find from the supplies she had brought in from China. This became the first step in her modus operandi for ministering to North Koreans. Esther quickly became known among all of the villagers. From the oldest to the youngest, all would come to the door and seek food from Esther. Many of those who came to eat would tell devastating stories. The most common was of near-starvation, such as eating no protein for an entire year except for one egg. Once the people could see, through her generosity, that she genuinely cared for them and began to trust her, she was able to tell many of them about the gospel.

The Sister from China

There was one well-known woman who knew how to sing and play the guitar, but had contracted tuberculosis. She also suffered from severe malnutrition because there simply wasn't enough food. To make matters worse, her husband beat her every day. By the time Esther met her, she had been reduced to a walking bag of bones. Her eyes were dim and she looked as if she would fall asleep at any minute and never wake up.

Esther could not believe that this woman had the strength to endure another beating from her husband. Esther fed her pork soup and white rice, which she ate with tears in her eyes. It seemed that she was gaining strength with each bite she took. She looked up at Esther with tear-filled eyes.

"Thank you so much for this food," she said. "I have not had meat in a very long time." She looked down and tried to remember the last time. "One time I wanted to eat meat so badly that I cooked a leather belt I had found on the street."

A few days later, the lady returned with her husband and nine-year-old son. Esther could see that they were also emaciated and starving, so she offered them some soup and rice. The husband was very reserved and reluctant to take anything offered to him, but he was also in survival mode and could not refuse free food. After he began eating, he opened up and started talking.

Esther found it relatively easy to talk with him. He said he had graduated from Pyongyang University, one of the most prestigious universities in North Korea. Esther found that they had a lot in common and could talk for a long time about their shared interests.

After a long conversation, Esther found an opportunity to share the gospel. As soon as she mentioned the name of Jesus, he grew quiet and listened intently. He seemed to soak up everything Esther was saying about this totally unknown Jesus. They left later that night and Esther did not see them again for a while.

One day, as she was walking back to the home she was staying at, she heard someone call her name. She turned and saw the singer with tuberculosis. When Esther stopped, the woman came running in full sprint and—in a gesture that is never seen in North Korea—wrapped her arms around Esther's neck.

"My sister from China!" she exclaimed. "I didn't know if I would ever see you again! It is so good to see you." Esther was shocked that this woman acted so lovingly in public.

"It is good to see you again as well," Esther replied. "How are things going with you and your husband?"

"Oh, they could not be better. I don't know what happened. He used to beat me, threaten my life, and make things miserable for our child, but now he is a changed man. He treats me nicer than he ever has before. It seems like he changed after you shared those words with him that night. I am just amazed by how much better things have gotten for me."

Esther rejoiced with her. "This is just the beginning," she said. "It only gets better," she said while gesturing upward to heaven, indicating that God had more in store for this woman and her husband.

CHAPTER 13

Confronting the Idols

Life in North Korea is full of walking. Only the rich can afford even a bicycle, and those are easily stolen. It was never safe to walk alone in North Korea, so Esther only walked in groups of people. This also gave her a chance to share with her disciples as they walked together. The deserted country roads provided the perfect opportunity for her to teach them about Christ, much like Christ Himself had done on the dusty Judean roads with His disciples during His earthly ministry.

One day while walking with a group of around five locals she had gotten to know quite well, she silently prayed against all the idols she saw around her. Idols for worshiping Kim Jong Il and Kim Il Sung are everywhere in the form of large photographs, propaganda posters, statues, and signs with slogans on them. Everywhere the North Koreans walked, they were surrounded with the idolatry. The group she was walking with was very interested in what she was doing, so Esther began to explain to them about the power of prayer as they listened eagerly. After a while, she walked with them off to the side of the road. Everywhere they walked was mud and water because it had just rained, but no one seemed to mind. They all stood in the muddy water while Esther led them to the Lord.

Another prayer that was frequently on Esther's lips as she walked from place to place was a plea for forgiveness for not understanding the North Korean people. She eventually realized that it was impossible for her to understand the local residents and their ways by her own wisdom. She was ashamed of her lack of understanding, even after so much time ministering there. At times she felt like Satan was going to swallow her up—like she was being attacked from all sides, but the attacks also seemed to be coinciding with each new level of favor that she gained. She reminded herself that Satan often attacks exactly where the Lord's work is being done.

Several businesses continued to contact her and use her as their main consultant in North Korea. They were excited to have such a zealous and knowledgeable representative in that mysterious country. North Korea was a black hole for most businesses. No one truly knew what went on inside, how to operate, or how to make money. Esther was an invaluable asset to them because she knew so much.

Esther wanted to connect with companies that produced food items so that she could have a way to make money as well as to help get food for her friends in North Korea. After some time she was able to connect with a noodle-making company, and they gave her a noodle machine to take into North Korea.

Esther took the noodle machine with her across the border and showed the local people how to set it up. The North Koreans had often tried to make noodles on their own, but they were not able to keep a regular noodle machine working because the squalid conditions caused the machines to rust, break down, and be impossible to repair. Local residents often had to buy their noodles from miles away because there were so few noodle makers.

The corn harvest was regularly quite meager and often produced crops unsuitable for making most corn-based products. The Great Leader Kim Jong Il did not know anything about farming but was always imposing his rules on the agricultural communities. His words and teachings were considered sacred and infallible, so when he told the people how to farm, the farmers were obligated to follow his instructions to the letter. This proved to be disastrous. Simple crops like corn that people had grown for generations proved almost impossible to produce because of Kim Jong Il's counterproductive guidance.

Noodles, however, are a corn-based product that can be made from the rougher parts of the corn plant. In order to make noodles, Esther first had to teach the people how to use every part of the corn, including the cob. This was hard with the machines, but possible. Esther was able to get a technician from China to come with her and show the locals how to use the machine in a way that would prolong the life of the equipment. The noodle machine was a huge hit! Everyone loved it and a lot of previously useless corn suddenly had a use.

Bow or Die?

The government officials soon took notice of the stir created by the noodle machine and even the local Party Secretary heard about the machine and came to visit her. He was impressed with the productivity she had brought to their area and wanted to invite her to an official dinner at the Chinese Consulate where many well-known officials from North Korea and China would be in attendance.

She politely refused the invitation, but the Party Secretary continued to insist. He even sent an official government car to pick her up. This was a huge honor, and it would have been politically disastrous to refuse.

"Esther, you have done many great things for the motherland," the Party Secretary said. The official kept heaping praises on her, and the driver continued to look back at her whenever he could. It was clear that the driver was proud to be driving for such an honorable person who was working hard to improve life for the North Korean people.

"Lord, please give me wisdom," she prayed silently. "I can't do anything apart from You."

Esther was not sure what the dinner would be like and had no idea whom she would meet. She was painfully aware that fame could quickly extinguish her ability to minister to ordinary people on the streets because it would entail closer supervision from the government.

After driving for some time they finally arrived at a bronze statue of Kim Il Sung. The driver stopped and everyone got out of the car. It was customary for officials to pay their respects to the large statues of the leaders and to bow before them in worship.

Esther began to pray frantically, knowing that this short moment could mean the end of her time in North Korea. If she refused to bow to the great leader in worship, she might be forced to leave North Korea or even be put in jail. Locals could even be executed for refusing to bow before the Great Leader's statue.

As they walked together toward the statute, Esther was still at a loss as to how to deal the situation. Everyone lined up shoulder to shoulder beside each other and prepared to begin the ceremony.

"Dear Lord, what do You want me to do?" Esther prayed silently. Then suddenly a surge of boldness filled her heart and she began to pray differently.

"Kim Il Sung, you are not the King of kings. You are not the Lord of lords. You were a horrible, evil leader and I command you in the name above all names to fall down and disappear!"

Everyone bowed in unison except Esther. She stood upright and stared directly at the bronze statue. "Fall down in acknowledgement of the one and only King of kings."

The statue did not fall physically, but it no longer held any power over Esther. No one really noticed that she had not bowed because they had all closed their eyes as they did so. After bowing several times, there were a few who finally noticed Esther still standing upright.

"Teacher?" one of the party members asked. (They often called her "teacher," as a sign of respect in the Korean culture.) "Why don't you bow when we come together and pray before our Great Leader?"

"Please understand," Esther started out slowly, "I don't know how to greet others by bowing down. After all, isn't it only a bronze statue? It isn't the Great Leader himself. He didn't make it; someone made it to remind them of him. The statue can't do anything to acknowledge that I have been here paying my respects. If I wanted to truly honor the Great Leader, wouldn't it be better to do something for him or his people directly? Which would be better for you, to follow the teachings of your leader and help those around you, or to come and bow to a statue that can't do anything for you, the people, or the Leader?"

The people around her pondered her words for a moment, and did not respond. Amazingly, from that day onward, they never again asked her to bow before the statue.

The Harvest Is Plentiful

After only a few trips to North Korea, Esther felt compelled to share the gospel with as many people as she could, but wasn't sure how to maximize her audience in such a closed country. Everywhere she looked there were people hurting, afraid, and looking for a way out of their misery. They were like people waiting to be saved in the midst of a raging storm. As she pondered her dilemma, it became clear that her past ministry to refugees had actually laid the perfect foundation for her evangelistic efforts in North Korea. Many of her refugee disciples had returned to their homeland with aid for their families, and they quickly became her eyes and ears for knowing when and who to preach the gospel to. This growing network of disciples consisted of trustworthy and reliable believers who humbly received and applied her biblical teaching. It was according to their advice that she would visit this home or that in the dead of night, being assured by her disciples that the hearts of those families were ripe for the gospel.

On the first night after deciding to expand her ministry, she headed out after most people had gone to bed. The lack of street-lights made it a bit scary for her, but also concealed her movement. The families she met were expecting her. It was safer to meet in the privacy of a home at night when no one else was around to listen.

She continued visiting homes from that night on. Esther would sometimes spend all night preaching in a home. Not many people had lamps, so they would use fabric from blankets that Esther had brought from China, twist a strip of the cloth into a makeshift wick, and dip it in cooking oil to burn for light.

"Do not expect anything from me," she would say. "I am not capable of helping anyone and have no power to rescue you from your problems. I don't have all the answers, but I know the Answer—Jesus, the living God. He is not dead like your former leader Kim Il Sung."

The people in the room gasped at the notion that their Great Leader was dead. The North Koreans taught that Kim Il Sung was not dead, but had become the eternal leader of the Korean people so that when a Korean died, they would be reunited with him. To Esther, that sounded more like a living hell than heaven. She was always careful not to bring up politics, but whenever necessary did not hesitate to point out that Jesus, not the North Korean leaders, was God.

"The God who lives can touch you where you need it the most. He can heal your broken heart. All you have to do is ask. Only the one true God can give you eternal life. Believe in Jesus with all your heart and only then can you be saved from eternal damnation. I have no material wealth, but if you look to the living God, He can meet your needs."

The people had never heard any teaching of this kind before. They were moved by Esther's boldness and passion. They were captivated by the fact that a woman was brave enough to defy the law of Kim Jong Il and to teach something other than the Party line.

"Accept the teachings of Jesus Christ which lead to life and joy. If you accept Him into your heart today, you can taste heaven— even here in North Korea. You can have joy even now. You don't have to wait until you are dead to have peace in your heart. You can have it today, even in this place."

Sometimes her words were accepted and the people would cry out for salvation, but often she was rejected. Esther always prayed that she would preach in the power of the Holy Spirit so that the words from the Holy Spirit would be heard instead of her own.

Esther could not help but to think of Jesus' words: *"The harvest is plentiful, but the laborers are few"* (Matthew 9:37). There were so many people in North Korea who were hungry both spiritually and physically, but there were not many people willing to share the Word of the Lord in that land.

Esther often felt alone. She didn't know of even one other person preaching in North Korea. When she went from door to door at night, she found an endless number of people who had never heard the gospel before. When she searched among the few foreign philanthropic organizations operating in the area, she only found Christians who were too afraid to share their faith. People were drowning all around them, and yet no one was willing to throw them the lifejacket they needed—the living gospel. She cried out to God, "Am I the only one here serving You? I feel like I am completely alone. Why have You sent me into this situation by myself? Why am I the only one following Your will here in North Korea?"

Then she remembered the words of God to Elijah when he was feeling sorry for himself after fleeing from Jezebel: *"I will leave seven thousand in Israel, all the knees that have not bowed to Baal"* (1 Kings 19:18).

The number of people that were accepting Jesus as their Lord and Savior was growing each night. Esther was exhausted yet excited; in fact, she was too excited to stop. The opportunity to preach the gospel in the world's most closed country was an immense privilege. After several people in one location came to Christ, she would return regularly to their homes and disciple them.

Some of those she discipled illegally crossed into China to be trained by her when she was there and would then smuggle goods across the border. They often brought Bibles back to North Korea to meet the demand of the growing church there.

Those who brought Bibles into North Korea would often literally bury them in the ground so that they would not be found. When no one was around they would dig them up, read them, and rebury them afterward. Bibles were often torn into several pieces and then buried in different areas to minimize the risk of losing all of God's Word at once if discovered. These believers were truly hungry for the Word of God.

CHAPTER 14

The Generous Gospel in a Closed Country

There were spies everywhere sent specifically to uncover the kind of illegal activities Esther was involved in, so she had to be extremely careful, but she continued her evening activities nonetheless. Some people began to complain about her to the authorities, but those who complained didn't know who she was, where she was from, where she lived, or anything else about her. Because she was from the Korean region of China, she spoke with an accent quite similar to the North Koreans she was ministering to and thus didn't stick out. The darkness also prevented people from being able to give a description of what she looked like to the police.

Esther had to be careful not to be too generous or give gifts to people in public during the day because that would give her away to the police who were looking for her. They would know right away that she was the one evangelizing from house to house at night. When beggar children came to her, she felt the need to give them money, but was not able to do so publicly. If she openly gave them money, the police would just come and take it away from them anyway. Again and again she reminded herself that if she wanted to help someone in North Korea, it was always best to do it in private with no one watching.

One day while walking through the market, Esther saw a young boy who was obviously starving. Nearby a man bought a bowl of hot steaming noodles for himself. As the man leaned over to smell the fresh noodles, the boy ran by and snatched a handful of noodles right out of the man's bowl.

The boy knew he was going to be punished and would have the noodles taken away from him if he didn't eat them immediately. He threw the fistful of steaming hot noodles into his mouth, feeling both pain and pleasure. The man grabbed the boy, held him by the neck with one hand, and punched him in the face with the other. The impact of the blows knocked the little boy's head back and blood went everywhere, but no one around reacted.

At the other end of the market a woman was squatting down in the mud and selling popcorn. Esther saw her, but her mind was still occupied with the little boy who had put a few noodles in his belly for the price of a painful bloody nose. The woman looked so pitiful squatting there in the mud that out of pity Esther bought some of the woman's popcorn, paying the woman more than the popcorn had cost. She tried to hide the amount of money that she gave the woman, but in ignorance the woman stretched out the crisp bill to see how much she got. Esther motioned to her with her hand to put it away, but the woman thought Esther was trying to cheat her and wanted to make sure the money was not fake.

When she saw how much it was, she started crowing over her newfound fortune, but the joy was short-lived. As soon as Esther turned to walk away, another lady ran over and tried to grab it out of the woman's hand before she had a chance to put it in her pocket and a ruckus ensued.

Desperation had turned normal people into animals. The North Korean government taught that people evolved from monkeys and that their value was only found in how much they could produce. This meant that someone was worthless if they could not produce much. The elderly and handicapped were thought of as dead weight in society. Children were only as valuable as their potential future production. Communism was the country's religion, the Leader was their god, and everything in North Korea seemed to be on the path of destruction because of this idolatry.

Esther could see clearly that idol worship was leading to more and more intense disease, poverty, and sorrow. Lung disease was widespread. Famine was everywhere. Even families with children were forced to abandon them, sell them, or eat them to survive. As a mother, the stories that people told to her night after night about their children were too much for her to handle. She would wake up from horrible nightmares and cry out to God for salvation for the people of North Korea. She persevered by her faith that God was going to answer those prayers in a mighty way.

Growing Risk

The more Esther ministered, the more people came to know Christ, but she was also aware that the more people came to Christ, the more exposed she was. It became difficult to know whether someone was genuinely accepting the teachings of Jesus or only pretending to in order to trap her. She could only trust in the Lord and believe that He would protect her. She listened to her North Korean friends when they told her to be careful. She relied on them when determining who to trust and who not to. Her life was in their hands.

Her only goal was to share with as many people as she could, knowing that the more people she could share the gospel with, the more people she could teach to treat each other with love and respect and share the gospel themselves.

The number of people accepting Jesus was growing to the point that it was no longer possible for Esther to visit and teach everyone. Even if she went to several houses per night, she was still not able to visit all her disciples even once a month. At the same time, she was not able to do the most logical thing and ask them to come together so that they could meet all at once because such a gathering could prove deadly. Families would often vanish if they were suspected of a crime. Sometimes authorities would use them as examples to teach a lesson to other citizens, but other times the entire family would simply disappear and never be heard from again.

The new believers began to ask many questions concerning the teachings they were receiving from Esther. "You said we should pay tithes on everything we have, right teacher?" one person asked.

"Yes, the Bible teaches us that we should honor the Lord with what we have and give ten percent."

"But we don't have much. We are barely surviving. Shouldn't we wait until we have more to live on before we give? The government already takes almost everything that we make. Aren't we exempt from this?"

"No," Esther replied with boldness. "God does not need your money. He does not need you to give ten percent. It is for your benefit, not His. The practice does not cease during your time of poverty. As children of God, we cannot be owned by the things of this world. We have to completely give them over to God and trust that He will supply all our needs according to His riches and glory."

"But where do we pay, teacher? We don't have a church we can give the money to. Do we give the money to you?"

This was more of a challenging question. Esther did not want to touch any money for fear that rumors would spread and pollute the message she had for the people. Because there were so many thieves and con men in North Korea, she did not want to be mistaken for someone who was after the money of the poor.

"You should take an offering in your homes whenever you meet. When you meet with me and when you meet alone, you should take up an offering and the money should be given to the people on the street. You should use it to help people, buy food for the least among you, or to pay the hospital bills of a fellow believer. Think of the poorest you know or whoever is in the most difficult situation, even if it is your enemy, take your gathered tithes, and go bless that person."

Sharing and giving to the disadvantaged does not make sense to North Koreans and is not practiced anywhere in their country. Only gifts to the Dear Leader make sense to the population. This was a completely new way of thinking for them. They had to step out of their comfort zone and give to others. Even though it was odd for them, there was something about it that seemed right.

"You are now children of God. You cannot steal. Even if it means starving to death, you cannot steal food. Rely upon God to provide for you without breaking His law. Everyone here is starving to death. You are all equally in need. One stolen bowl of cornmeal is not going to keep you alive anyway. If you are starving to death, you will still die, but it is better to die from being honest and loving toward others than to die while stealing food from someone else."

Esther continued working hard to get people Bibles, but she feared that she would be caught and deported from North Korea before people would receive them. There was no way to get Bibles into the hands of all the people who needed them.

In addition to burying them under the ground, some of her disciples would bury their Bibles underneath the ashes in the fireplace where they would cook their meals. They would put all the ashes into a container, dig deep into the ground under the fireplace so that the Bible wouldn't be damaged by the fire's heat, and then bury it underneath the ashes they would pour back out of the container.

When Esther arrived at some of the homes at night, the families would dig out their Bibles, and then they would pray, sing softly, and read from the Bible together.

The number of people she was able to meet with on one evening was small and there simply weren't enough evenings, so Esther began to meet with some families during the day. The families would send their children out to play, and if the children saw anyone coming they could alert their parents in enough time for them to hide their activities.

Answered Prayers

Only the most trusted families were allowed to hold meetings together with Esther during the day. Those families put boards and objects over the windows so that no one was able to see in from outside. They would also use the most remote room in the house so that passersby on the street could not hear the sound of their meeting. Esther saw much fruit from her ministry. Broken families were restored and children dying of diseases were miraculously healed. One person who was coughing up blood with a deadly case of tuberculosis was immediately healed in response to prayer. One child suffering from convulsions that regularly caused him serious injury was healed during prayer and never had another convulsion. Home after home was experiencing the power of the living God and undeniable miracles were taking place.

"There are museums for your leaders and you are worshipping their idols, but people are dying all around you day and night," she would preach passionately. "In front of you there is a cliff. You are standing on a ledge that drops directly into the pits of hell. Look around, every day people are walking off that cliff. There are people jumping off the ledge and plunging to their death. People are dying from murder, disease, and starvation, but you still pray to the idols made in the image of the ones who have brought this death upon you. However, you are not without hope. You are not without a chance to change. You can stretch out your hands right now and receive Jesus. He is here waiting to receive you. He is the only One who can give you salvation," she would tell them.

"My Father controls the entire universe. He made you. He designed you in specific detail to be the most precious child for Him. He wants to love you and care for you with the love of a Father."

One night Esther visited the family of a young lady she had led to Christ in China. The daughter had come back and forth to China a few times to get supplies and to study the Bible at Esther's house. When Esther went to their home in North Korea, they told her that they would like to follow the teachings of Jesus, but that it was impossible to live in North Korea without lying.

Esther understood what they were saying and realized that they were babes in Christ, but told them emphatically that a Christian must do away with lying, cheating, stealing, killing, adultery, and even the thoughts of those acts.

"God knows your needs. He knows what you are lacking. He knows how to provide His children with the daily bread they need to live. The Bible says that if you knock, the door will be opened for you. Ask and you will receive. I promise you, God will not fail you."

After one month, Esther returned to their home. She knocked on their door with bags of rice, flour, and a few other necessities in her arms. The daughter answered the door and immediately threw her arms around Esther's neck.

"Praise God for you!" she sobbed. "We have not had anything to eat for two days. We wanted to steal corn from a neighbor's fields, but we didn't. We didn't know what to do so we prayed. We have been praying for two days for food and now we see that God has used you to answer our prayers."

This was but one example of the incredible faith of these new believers. The secret fellowships were really showing promise. Esther looked around and felt that there were at least twenty-five fellowships that could play a key role in building up the country if the regime fell. It seemed like a lofty thought, but she was certain that these twenty-five underground house churches were like anchors that had been planted in the ground as a future foundation for a country that desperately needed to start over.

CHAPTER 15

Paper Tigers

One day the local government in the North Korean township where Esther often stayed called her in for questioning. They asked her what she was doing, why she was in North Korea, and why she continued to come back time after time. At first, her frequent visits to North Korea had been welcome, but apparently now the local officials were starting to get suspicious of her. They allowed her to return to where she was staying, but called her in on several occasions after that and would spend long periods of time asking her the same questions she had already answered when she crossed the border.

Every time they questioned her, they also demanded food and money from her. Their questioning started to become more and more intense. Everywhere Esther went, she knew that she was being followed. As the pressure increased, she became just as suspicious of the local authorities as they were of her.

Somehow the authorities were able to identify all of the twenty-five families that Esther had been visiting and had considered to be strategic to the future of the church. The police interrogated each family thoroughly. All the families claimed ignorance, except for three men in three of those families who boldly professed their faith in Christ.

"She Taught Us to Pray"

Their courage and fortitude shocked the entire community. No one had ever made such a bold declaration of faith to the authorities before. All three of the men were dragged out of their homes, paraded in front of their neighbors, and then beaten and put in prison. Authorities tortured the three of them until they gave up more information.

The police would beat people for more information, but once they got it, they would beat the people even more to punish them for keeping secrets from the government, and death would soon follow. The officials had no use for people once they had fulfilled their purpose. Life had no value to them and they did not serve out of a need for justice or honor, but merely used the job to secure their own positions in the community.

The information that the three men shared led the police to go back and interrogate others. They went from door to door, seeking out the same homes that Esther had visited night by night.

The police went after the children first, knowing that they were the easiest to frighten into talking. In the first home, one of the officers grabbed a five-year old child and held him by the neck.

"You little runt, what do you know about Jesus?" he snarled. The child was crying for his mother, but the mother couldn't do anything but watch.

"Don't look at your mother. Look at me. Who told you about Jesus?" The little child urinated down his leg out of fear and urine splattered all over the ground and on the arm of the officer. The officer then threw the child toward the door.

"Get out!" he shouted. "Get out of my sight before I kill you!" The officer marched into the living room and peered down at the mother who was squatting in a corner on the dirt floor of her poorly lit home.

"What was the Chinese woman doing here? Did she tell you about Jesus? Is she giving you money and proselytizing you? I want answers and I am not leaving here until someone starts talking."

"She taught us how to pray," the husband said in a low whisper. The officer quickly spun around on his heels and went over to the husband.

"What did you say?"

"I said that she taught…" the husband chose his words carefully, knowing that giving up information rarely got anyone out of trouble.

"…she taught us to pray."

"Pray? Pray to whom? Who did she teach you to pray to?"

"She taught us to pray for food. When we were sick, she taught us to pray for good health."

The police officer gripped his club with both hands and swung it violently at the husband. It hit his back, and the husband fell to his knees in pain.

"What? You let her teach you these lies? You let her teach your family these lies? What kind of man are you? You are a coward! You are not a revolutionary for your country. You are a shame to the Dear Leader."

Another officer came running into the room.

"Your child is saying that the woman from China taught you to pray," he said. "Who did you pray to?" He raised his club in the air while demanding more answers. "Who did you pray to?"

"We were taught to pray when things were bad," the husband continued. "We were taught to pray even when things were good. The woman from China told us that we should not run away from our country, but we should pray for our country. She taught us to study hard in school, to work hard, and to be honest. She taught us to not steal or lie."

"Who did she teach you to pray to?" the officer shouted in a fury. The husband was reluctant to answer, but the officers were ready to beat him and his family to a bloody pulp unless he replied.

"You will answer him," one of the officers shouted after hitting the husband on the back with his club again.

"Jesus!" The man shouted with a defeated voice forced from the blow to the back. "She told us to pray to Jesus." The officers went around from home to home and got the same story from many families. Even the children were beaten until they told the officers what they wanted to hear. No one was exempt from their investigation.

Under Interrogation

In the evening, a car pulled up outside of the house where Esther was staying. Inside it were three officials wearing black suits—the clothing of choice for members of the government security bureau. They got out of the car and stood outside the door, yelling for Esther.

When she came out, one of the men in a black suit instructed Esther to get in the car with them to answer some questions. Esther knew that her compliance was mandatory. They were actually being very restrained by not physically forcing her into the car.

Esther recognized the driver from one of the homes she had visited at night. She had preached at his house and he had received

Jesus. Wanting to protect his secret, she didn't acknowledge him or speak to anyone. She just sat in the back seat and began to pray silently.

They eventually drove up to a big steel gate. Someone behind the gate opened it by hand and the gate clicked behind them as soon as they drove through. Esther was brought into a small room with an old sofa and a black-suited officer sitting at a desk. She had never seen him before. Lying on the desk in front of him was a stick about a yard long. Before she could ask any questions or make any determinations, he began to curse her and to accuse her of all kinds of crimes.

"What are you doing here?" he demanded. "Are you spreading your lies in the village? Are you tricking people here in our country like you did to the refugees in China? Why are you breaking the law and trying to twist peoples' minds?"

As he barked at Esther and slammed a club on the table, he expected her to be intimidated. He was used to people sitting in front of him and begging for mercy. But instead of fearing him, Esther yelled right back.

"How dare you accuse me of twisting the minds of your people?" She pointed her finger at him. "I gave my own food to your people when they came to me hungry, sick, and tired. I gave them rice and noodles from the mouths of my own family. What have you done?" She stood up and slammed her fists on the desk. "Pyongyang asked me to come over the border because I have done nothing but good things for this country!"

The interrogator was shocked. No one in the room was used to anyone being so bold when they were brought in for questioning. Esther even surprised herself with her courage. She could act in that way because the Lord had enabled her to see that these men were mere paper tigers. They could growl and bare their claws at her all they wanted, but even the slightest puff of wind from God's throne could blow them over in an instant.

"You are a Christian," he responded in an accusatory tone.

"So what? What is the problem with being a Christian? Are there not churches in Pyongyang? If there was a problem with being a Christian, would there be a church in your own capital city? The Great Leader's mother was a Christian, would you say that the mother of this nation's founder was an evil person?"

Esther impressed herself, but she was in for a long week ahead and only realized it after she had been in the interrogation room for a whole day. Several men kept coming in and yelling at her, constantly throwing accusations at her all day long. After a while, Esther's argument, which sounded so justified and rational in the beginning, started to fade. No one understood her logic because each one of them had been programmed by the government to block out all outside information. Their minds were like impenetrable walls and Esther was not able to get through. One of the main officers leading the interrogation placed a paper in front of Esther and demanded that she sign it with her thumbprint.

"What is this?" demanded Esther.

"Put your thumb in the ink and place your print here," the officer barked back.

"What is it? I want to read it." The officer would not let her read what was written.

"How can I possibly confess to something if I don't know what I am confessing to?"

"You will sign this paper. Do you understand me? You will sign this paper in ink or blood." Esther was even more emboldened by that statement. She was not going to be coerced into signing her own death warrant. The stubbornness she had developed as a young girl came to the surface and the officials realized that they were not going to convince her to do anything by using threats.

After more than a week in jail, they were still not able to get Esther to sign the confession. The officials were stressed. Esther saw that they were in fact more stressed than she was. They raged like they had all the power in the world, but they were just as vulnerable as she was. They knew full well that if they did not produce the results their superiors demanded, they could very easily end up in the same place she was: behind bars. Eventually the officers began to change their tone with Esther. They needed her to sign the confession for their own security.

"Please sign this confession," they asked. "If you don't sign this confession, we could possibly lose everything. Our bosses are not going to be happy with us and our families could be in danger."

"I can only sign something that is truthful," Esther respond steadfastly. "What you are asking me to sign is not the truth."

They questioned her every day from seven in the morning until noon for the next six weeks. They did not give her any food or water during the time of the interrogation. A new person questioned her every other day so that every day the interrogator was fresh and full of new ideas of how to extract information from her. No one listened to anything she said unless she was telling them something they wanted to hear. They were like machines programmed to follow an agenda and incapable of following any other line of logic than what had been taught to them.

Slowly, Esther withdrew completely. She realized that it was not productive to spend energy arguing with anyone or showing the flaws in their logic. She realized that her war was not with flesh and blood, but with the spirit. Esther began to pray continually. It was the only way that she was going to survive the ordeal.

"Where did you go? I want to know all of the homes that you visited," one of the interrogators demanded. "I want to know who you met and who you preached to."

The Bible verse telling her not to fear kept flashing through her mind. *You are my precious child and I will lead you and guide you,* a voice said to Esther's spirit. She could feel the presence of God with her, protecting her. She was instantly encouraged.

"When you were in China, why did you take refugees into your home? This is an act of hostility toward our country, do you realize that?" said the interrogator.

They wrote down her every reaction to their questions. From time to time they would put their written records down on the table and demand that Esther sign the notes, but she refused to. After only a short glance, it was clear to her that what was written on the papers was all false. One interrogator took his notepad, turned it toward Esther and told her to sign it. She glanced at it, grabbed it from the table, tore it in half, and tossed it into the air. "Who do you think you are?" the interrogator snapped. "I am not a person who agrees to lies," Esther retorted. Just then the door opened and officers walked in with a stack of folders and papers.

"You are not one to lie, hmm?" asked the officer rhetorically. "What we have here are records of all the times your name has come up during investigations and questioning. These files represent a couple of years. So, you see, we have been watching you and collecting information on you. We know who you are and what you have been doing. We know everything about you. We are only giving you a chance to tell us the truth to make this process easier on you."

They had dates, names, and locations of people who had been coming to her house in China for help as well as those whom she had been assisting in North Korea. They also had written testimonies from people she had been ministering to inside North

Korea. Esther could only imagine what the people must have gone through to compel them to sign those confessions.

Then a top-ranking official walked into the room. He looked at the ripped-up testimony on the floor and sighed in disapproval as he walked by her. Esther was certain that this was the beginning of the end. Offending the officers by ripping up their documents was a major offense; she was sure she would not exit the prison alive.

Esther looked down at the floor and shook her head silently back and forth as if to argue with herself about whether or not she should say something. Everyone else scurried out of the room in a manner that would not offend the senior officer. It was clear that the officers were afraid of him.

The Senior Officer

With only the senior officer and Esther in the room, she broke the silence. "You can kill me, but I will never deny Jesus Christ. Remember this: if I die, I will go to heaven, but if you die without receiving Jesus as your Lord and Savior you will most certainly go to hell. You might live longer than me in this world, but this world is only a whisper compared to eternity."

The officer looked at Esther and did not try to stop her from preaching. Esther expected to be stopped and had not planned to say more, but when he remained quiet, she figured that she might as well continue and shared about the love of Jesus and how much North Korea desperately needed it. Then she did the unthinkable. She looked the officer in the eye and told him, "The North Korean people need Jesus. Even you, sir, need to accept Jesus as your Lord and Savior. You cannot continue the life of pain and sorrow you are living any longer. You cannot keep denying the truth that you already know in your heart. Jesus loves you and is speaking to you right now."

She paused for a moment. "You can accept Jesus Christ into your life and He can bring you everlasting peace." Esther had nothing to lose. At that moment she had put it all on the line. If she was going to die, it was going to be because she had shared the gospel. She did not want to die and stand before Jesus only to realize that she had had a chance to see one more person come to Christ but had not taken it.

Esther looked up at him. Instead of being angry, he really seemed to be listening intently to every word she was saying. His eyes were focused on her and he was attentive. When she had finished speaking, the officer calmly stood and paced around the desk. "Can you return here tomorrow at 8 a.m.?" he said. Esther was a bit confused about what he had just said. She thought that her ears were playing tricks on her.

"Yes. I can return tomorrow at eight," she replied.

"Good, but before you go, I will need you to agree to sign a confession for your crimes."

"I cannot agree to sign any confession that I have not written out myself."

"Very well," he replied. "Write out the laws of China and North Korea, confess to the crimes that you committed in China when you assisted the North Korean refugees, and complete the document before morning."

"Very well," Esther said.

With that he dismissed her with a wave of his hand.

She was confused, but was not going to ask for clarification from him. She wanted to leave quickly, but her legs could barely walk. She had spent so many days under intense interrogation and without proper food and water that her body and mind were extremely weak. She stood and hobbled down the hall, but was so faint that when she got to the door of the prison, she could no longer see.

Off in the distance, just far enough away to avoid being noticed, several of Esther's disciples were waiting in the darkness. They had abandoned all thoughts of self-preservation and had been waiting outside the prison for several weeks, praying for her to come out. As soon as she walked out the door, they ran to her, and Esther collapsed right into the arms of those waiting for her. They quietly carried her back to the place where she was staying. It had been a tough battle.

And yet there were still more to come.

CHAPTER 16

A Blessing in Disguise

Esther later learned that she had been released at the request of a government official. A Chinese delegation was coming to town to meet with high-level North Korean government officials and the North Koreans could not find anyone to interpret for them. As much as they wanted to punish Esther for her actions, they also needed her assistance. Esther could speak both languages, knew official protocol, and had been making a lot of progress in improving the business climate in the area. She was the perfect person for the job. The only problem was that at that point, she was being held as a prisoner.

If she told the delegation, her fellow Chinese citizens, that she was actually a prisoner in North Korea, the situation could become very bad for the government officials because they would lose face. Therefore, they decided to use her imprisonment as a bargaining chip to secure her cooperation. Esther agreed to help interpret for the government officials and promised not to mention that she was a prisoner. In turn, the officers promised that she would have favor in her case and might be able to get an early release.

Because the government needed her help, Esther hoped for their mercy. She had learned that about twenty people had been captured in North Korea while trying to sneak back into the country from China, five of whom had Bibles. The five with Bibles were taken to the town square and made into a public spectacle. A government official read their crimes aloud to everyone and announced their punishment. After the charges and the sentences were declared, several soldiers brought out hammers and repeatedly struck the heads of the accused until they died. The word of their brutal execution had gone out to all of the surrounding towns soon after.

The problem that the authorities had was that they could not use Esther to make the statement that Christianity would not be tolerated in the country if she were allowed to go free. The officials knew too much about her to feign ignorance about her activities, and those in the villages knew too much as well. The same government officials who had needed her help were also responsible for publicizing her arrest as a warning to others.

On the night of her initial release, Esther's friends carried her to their house and provided the most elaborate meal they could for her.

"What is going on? What is all of this for?" she asked.

"We are just so happy that you are alive," they replied.

This was not the first time that Esther had seen such signs of devotion and sacrifice from the locals. How touching it was for her to see over and over that the love of Christ had not only penetrated their hearts, but had obviously changed their lives.

Esther was not sure what awaited her the next day, so she sent a message to her family in China that if she did not return within a week or so, she was probably dead. She hoped the interpreting work she provided for the government would be enough to buy her some goodwill, but she also knew that the government could not be trusted in any deal. Once they got what they wanted, they would mostly likely forget all about their promises.

Esther's husband got the message in China about her situation and immediately contacted other missionaries to seek help, but they all rejected him because they were too afraid that they would be connected to Esther's activities if they got involved. Many of them even slammed the door in his face and told him to never contact them again.

With no one willing to help him, Esther's husband traveled to the border alone and waited by the river, weeping every day. He felt completely helpless because there was nothing he could do to protect his dear wife.

When Esther's mother realized that her daughter might be executed in North Korea, she began to pray. "If my daughter is dead, then I might as well be dead too," she said to all those around her when she heard the news. Esther's mother and several other believers gathered together and prayed for many days.

A Prayer in the Darkness

The night was coming to an end and Esther knew that she had to finish writing a confession before morning for the senior official. She knew that her life would depend on what she wrote or didn't write. In the back of her mind she wondered if her confession would be sent to the Chinese government, knowing that China was just as dangerous for her as North Korea and that the Chinese government would not think twice about executing her or sentencing her to life in prison.

At around two o'clock in the morning, the pressure was getting to be too much for her, so she walked into the dark outside. Her feet were swollen from the long walks she had been forced to make to police station for interrogation every day. Each step was accompanied by pain.

The moon and stars hid themselves from the sky that night. No light could be seen at all in the sky. Esther held her hand in front of her face but couldn't see it. As hard as it was to walk in such darkness, she needed to lose herself in prayer, away from any distractions. Prayer was the only thing she could hold on to that would allow her to keep her sanity. Everything else was falling apart.

She walked into the dark until she bumped into a tree. She wrapped her arms around the tree and began to weep. "Thank You, God!" she cried. "Thank You for everything. Thank You for the wonderful opportunity I have had to minister to the people here. Thank You for the honor of carrying Your name into the darkest place on earth. It seems that my journey is now over. I just want to be united with You. If You have ever listened to my prayer, listen to this one—bring me home. Have mercy on me this one last time and bring me home to You."

She hugged the tree, closed her eyes, and felt the fullness of the Holy Spirit within. She began to sing. In that moment she felt the peace and joy of serving God and knew that all would be well with her soul, no matter what might happen to her body.

The War Veteran

Before the sun came up, Esther began her walk back to the police station, praying every step of the way. The bottoms of her feet were still swollen. Before she got to the road, a man approached her, desperate to speak with her.

"Please, sister, can we talk?" he said as he pulled out a paper that identified him as a very important person. Esther thought that he was probably working with the police. The paper he held in his hand identified him as a "revolutionary patriotic martyr," the highest honor for a North Korean which was reserved only for war veterans.

Esther didn't answer, but gestured that they could talk.

The man said quickly with tears in his eyes, "You don't know me, but I have heard about you. I don't know where to turn. Please give me a few minutes." For a North Korean war hero to be crying in front of a foreign woman was no small thing. But at that moment his pain was more powerful than his shame.

"I dug out a small farm to make a living from. With my own two hands, I dug out a plot of farmland on the side of the mountain, but after I had done all the work and prepared the land, the government came and told me that everything I harvest will belong to them." He looked down at his revolutionary patriotic martyr certificate. "This award meant nothing to them."

He cried and squeezed Esther's hands. Esther did not know what to do. Perhaps he was a spy sent to get additional information to incriminate her.

Esther pulled away and prayed. She was not sure what to do. Sharing the gospel with a man while under investigation could be treasonous, but not praying with a man who was reaching out for help would be like slapping God in the face.

Esther held out her hands and took hold of his. She then told him about Jesus Christ. She looked into the eyes of this humble man who had served the Communist regime faithfully for more than seventy years but had nothing left but desperation and hopelessness. After only a few moments of sharing with him about the love and power of Christ, she asked him if he wanted to receive Jesus. He nodded yes and received Jesus Christ as his Lord and Savior right there on the roadside.

Esther promised to meet him again in heaven, but for now, she had to hurry to the police station.

The End of a Nightmare

That day, Esther's life changed completely—again. To the amazement of all her friends and family, from the moment that she handed in her written confession, she was taken on as an official translator for the regime while they held important meetings with Chinese officials. God began to move in a powerful way among the officials. One of them visited Esther every day to give her a special Korean dog meat soup, traditionally believed to provide energy and vitality. The nourishment her body needed was being provided by her enemies! All Esther could do was praise God in response.

Her nightmare was slowly ending. She still did not know if she would be allowed to outlive her usefulness to the government, but she had a special serenity that surpassed any fear that tried to creep into her mind. Early one morning before seven o'clock, a security bureau car pulled up in front of the place where she was staying on house arrest. There was a plaque in the front of the car, marking the vehicle as a special gift from Kim Jong Il. That plaque gave the driver and anyone in the vehicle special access to any area in North Korea.

"Get in please," spoke someone from inside the vehicle.

"*Please?*" she thought to herself. "What is this all about?" After about five weeks of being tortured and interrogated, this was the first time anyone had ever used such respectful language with her.

Esther climbed into the car only to find that several of the people who had interrogated her and threatened to kill her were inside. The senior officer spoke first. "Esther, I hope that your experience in the motherland has not been completely ruined. I further hope that we can be friends. It is my deepest desire that I maintain a lifelong friendship with you."

Esther couldn't believe what she was hearing. Was this actual emotion and sincerity coming from the top official in charge of her case? The car drove north on the bumpy dirt road and swirls of dust followed behind. The other officials said some things and Esther pretended to listen, but was actually trying to keep track of where they were headed. She recognized landmark after landmark and knew that this was a road she had taken herself many times before. They were heading toward the China border.

When they arrived, the other officials got out of the car first and opened the door for Esther. They stood perfectly still while watching the woman they had held captive for over a month climb out of the vehicle. The officer again asked, "Do you have any last words or thoughts that you would like to leave with us before you return home? This is most likely the last time we will meet here in the motherland."

Esther considered the weight of that moment. She was being allowed to walk back across the bridge to freedom in China, and her mind was racing. "There are many things that I do not understand," Esther began, as they stood there together at the border.

Esther always crossed the border back into China wearing different clothes than she had come in with. She wore as many clothes as she could when entering North Korea, along with lots of accessories such as rings and watches, so that she could donate and exchange them with needy locals and wear their old ragged clothes back to China. This time was no different. Nothing that she was wearing belonged to her. They were old, thin rags that she had received from a friend whom she had given her clothing to. But she stood tall with dignity.

"I might be back or I might not, but please know that the people of this country will always be welcome in my home no matter where I live. As long as I have a roof over my head and food in my home, there will always be a place at my table for North Koreans. I have been called by God to serve this nation and I will continue to do that until I am no longer able."

She bowed low to the officials, turned, and walked away. As she walked down the hill toward the bridge between China and North Korea, she could feel their eyes watching her. She wondered what they were thinking. She wondered if they would ever again think about the Jesus of whom she had preached to them and if she would ever see any of them again.

Back in China

When she arrived at the other side of the border, Chinese immigration officers immediately challenged her. They could see that she had overstayed her visa in North Korea. They knew that something had happened, but were not sure what.

The Chinese immigration officer in charge of her line was hot-tempered and quickly lost his patience with her. Esther could see she was in for a rough time. At the same time, a Chinese government official from Shenyang passed through the line. Esther recognized him right away, and he readily walked over to her with a smile.

"What are you doing here?" he asked. His smile quickly turned to confusion as he took in her ragged clothes, matted hair, and emaciated body. Esther looked like she had been through hell and back.

"What are you doing here?" he asked again, surprised and concerned.

"This young man is giving me a hard time about a visa that is none of his concern," Esther said loudly enough for everyone to hear. "This visa is for North Korea. I have worked out my complications with them over the matter, but now he has taken it upon himself to become a North Korean immigration officer instead of minding his own business."

"Here," the Shenyang official said, showing the immigration officer his credentials. "Let her go and if anyone asks you questions, you send them to me."

Immediately the officer stamped Esther's passport.

"Thank you so much," Esther said.

"No problem. Just buy me lunch sometime when you are in town."

The very system of corruption and networking relationships that Esther disliked was the same system that came to her rescue at that moment. The system of networking in China, or *guanxi*, as it's called, could hurt you or help you at any given moment. Whatever the law said was always secondary to who your contacts were and how much power they held in the spider's web of political relationships in government.

Esther gratefully walked out the doors of the immigration office, and immediately saw a man sitting quietly outside the main immigration checkpoint, staring across the river as if captured in a daze. It was her husband. Esther walked straight toward him, but he did not see her or recognize her. She got closer and called out his name. He turned to watch her approach, but still he could not accept that it was Esther. He thought she was a crazy North Korean trying to get his attention. She was limping, less than half the size he remembered, and wearing baggy old clothing that hung on her body like a sack.

Esther did not know it at the time, but her husband had not expected her to walk across the bridge. He was waiting for her body to be sent across in a box. Sure that she had been executed, her loyal husband wanted to be there when her body was transported back across the border.

She kept walking and called out his name again. He squinted against the sun, and suddenly recognized who she was. He almost ran out of his shoes as he rushed toward her. Wrapping his arms around her, he felt like he was going to break her in two because of her small size. He pushed her away enough to get a better look at her, and then embraced her again.

"And our son?" Esther asked with joy. "Let's go home to our son."

Esther might one day be martyred for her commitment to the gospel, but this was not that day.

CHAPTER 17

New Trials

Recovery took longer than Esther had expected. Weakened by her ordeal in North Korea, she was hit by several illnesses all at once. She reached out to a few foreign missionaries in the area but, as had been the case before, they were not willing to help her. Her incarceration in North Korea had made her a marked woman among the missionary communities in China, and no one wanted to have anything to do with her.

Once again Esther and her family had no one to turn to but God. She had to completely rely on the Word of God and be faithful to her calling. Even before she completely recovered, she was already back in action serving the refugee community in China, as if she had never left China. The days she had spent under interrogation in North Korea seemed like a distant memory, but sometimes her dreams were filled with the images of what she had endured.

Refugees were visiting her home day and night. During the icy cold months of January, when the river froze solid so refugees could easily cross over, their numbers started to increase rapidly.

It was early 2007, and Esther's refugee ministry was back in full operation.

An Unexpected Visit

One day she returned from the public bathhouse to teach a North Korean sister how to cook meals that she would also be able to cook back in North Korea. That day's menu was marinated lotus root.

Esther's husband had stepped out to buy some tofu. He had just departed when there was a knock on the door. Esther thought it was her husband returning because he had forgotten something. Without thinking, she flipped the latch and opened the door wide.

Immediately nine policemen burst through the door and pushed Esther back into the room.

"Esther?" one of the police officers asked sternly. "We have a warrant for your arrest," he said as he flashed a piece of paper in front of her. "Who is here in your house?" His goons began searching with place without waiting for an answer.

Esther's mind was spinning. Her home was a treasure trove of information for the police. They were searching from room to room, but no one had laid a hand on her yet. Without thinking, Esther swiftly moved past one of the doors and into her bedroom where her dresser was. The top drawer of her dresser contained a notebook with a list of all the North Korean refugees who had been coming to her house for help. She also had pictures, names, missionary contact information, and teaching materials in that top drawer. If those things were to fall into the wrong hands, many lives would instantly be in danger.

There wasn't a moment to lose. She opened the drawer, grabbed as much documentation as she could with both hands, spun around on one foot, pushed two guards out of the way, and ran for an open window. She launched the papers and pictures out into the busy street where they were quickly trampled into the snow below.

The police officers closest to her then tackled her to the ground and arrested her. They found her mobile phone in her pocket and confiscated it as evidence. Even though they saw with their own eyes how she threw the papers and pictures out of the window, they still did not recognize what she did. It was as if God had blinded their eyes.

After securing her, they stood her back up and led her out the door. Her son sat by helplessly as his mother was once again taken away. All the refugees who were in her apartment were arrested as well. One of them was even handcuffed to her. Only Esther's mother and son were left in the apartment.

Black Jail

The officers put Esther in a car together with the refugee she was handcuffed to and drove them to a small motel close to the train station. Motels and abandoned apartment buildings are often used in China to temporarily hold and interrogate religious leaders. When Christians are officially incarcerated, they can cause problems for China because international observers often obtain records of their imprisonment, so the Chinese police have formed an elaborate system of underground jails and detention centers known as "black jails." These makeshift jails are scattered all over China and have been used to secretly detain several hundred thousand people without warrants or family notification. Many black jail detainees vanish without a trace so that no one can make any claims of torture or maltreatment.

Although this was Esther's first black jail experience, she knew that China did many things to cover up persecution of Christians, which is why she never expected China to help her when she was held in North Korea. When they arrived at the motel, guards were posted outside the door and the windows were covered so that no one could see in or out.

The officer in charge pulled a large pile of files out of his brief-case and laid it on the desk before her. Esther sat in front of the officer, uncomfortably handcuffed to the North Korean refugee who didn't understand any of the Chinese being spoken. The room was not big enough for many people to be in at once and the light-ing was dim in the cigarette-smoke-filled air.

"Here is a collection of records of about seven years of your bad behavior, Esther." Two men stood on each side of her as she sat looking at the files. "Seven years, Esther. We have been watch-ing you and following you, and today you are going to tell us everything."

Esther sat there silently.

"How long have you been involved in Christian ministry?" he asked. Esther didn't answer. "How long have you been preaching your antigovernment propaganda about Jesus?" Again, Esther didn't say anything. "How long have you been assisting criminals from North Korea?"

"I don't know anything about criminals from North Korea," Esther replied, "but if you are referring to people I have met on the streets here in China who needed my help…then yes, I have offered my assistance to them."

The officer was not ignorant of what Esther had been up to. He knew a lot of names and details, and his questions got more and more aggressive. After about an hour of interrogation, someone knocked on the door. It was one of the officers posted outside. The door opened and they brought in a poor, ragged gentleman who was also a refugee from North Korea, one of Esther's disciples.

"Here is a friend of yours that you might recognize," the officer said, pointing to the North Korean brother. "We just caught him and some other North Koreans trying to illegally cross the border of China back into North Korea. He sang like a bird," the officer said. The brother they arrested was a good Christian whom Esther had led to the Lord, but he was not a very good criminal. He was an open book and shared too much information.

"Sorry, Esther. They told me that I needed to pay them money if I wanted to be released, so I told them to call you because you might be able to help. I never suspected that…" he babbled, trying to quickly explain the situation so that Esther would not get angry at him.

"Shh…it's ok," Esther assured him.

"I never knew that they would arrest you too, Esther. I honestly didn't know," he finished.

"No. It's ok," Esther assured him again. She knew that he had good motives and that none of this was his fault. After an hour of interrogation, Esther's adrenaline levels began to crash and she started to shiver. There was no heat in the hotel and it was twenty degrees below zero, Celsius. The floor was made of concrete and it seemed to radiate the chill straight through her body.

"So you see, Esther, resistance and feigned ignorance are not going to get you anywhere. All of the evidence we need is already right here in this room. We have enough evidence to push for the death sentence. Your only hope is to cooperate and pray that we are lenient toward you."

Esther calmly looked up at the officer in charge. If the North Korean officials couldn't scare her, then these officers in China did not stand a chance. The occasional silence in the room was broken by the sound of a train passing by outside. After a few hours in the small motel room, Esther and the refugee she was handcuffed to were led to the train station. They were then surrounded by an escort of nine police officers who took them to a secure train car and made them board.

"Where are we going?" Esther asked one of the officers.

"Shut your mouth!" he barked back. "Do not say a word and don't ask questions!"

They marched up the ramp into the train car. The train had windows every half meter, but they were all covered. Once on the train, Esther walked up to one of the windows and tried to see if she could move a curtain to look out the window. Immediately one of the officers smacked her hand.

"Touch it again and I will break your hand. Do you understand?" The officer spoke to Esther like she was a child. The refugee handcuffed to Esther was a young North Korean girl who didn't have enough clothes on to protect her from the cold. She was shivering both from the cold and from fear.

"Esther? I am scared. What are they going to do to us?"

"Shut up!" yelled the officer. "No talking." The officer shoved them down onto a hard bed where they were able to sit, and then handcuffed Esther's free hand to the bar of the bed.

The train's horn signaled that it was time to leave, and Esther wished she even knew the direction they were heading. She was alone; her family had no way of identifying the black jail she had been held in or of now knowing she was on a train. Her mind went through the possibilities of getting in contact with them, but came up empty.

The young North Korean girl could not stop crying. She was in a strange country with a different language and culture, completely clueless about everything going on around her. She was not a criminal, but a victim of Kim Jong Il and his policies that left his people starving. This young girl had only been trying to find a way to survive.

Esther watched the guards until the train rocked them to sleep. Then she leaned back and positioned herself so that the young lady handcuffed to her could rest her head on her shoulder and have her ear next to Esther's mouth. Esther slowly began to whisper to her, "Don't worry, God will take care of us. Just be strong and believe in Him. I have seen Him pull me through situations much more difficult than this one. He has never failed me and He will never fail you."

"Stop talking," one of the officers said as he peeked through one open eye. But Esther quietly continued to minister to the girl. She knew that the officers did not speak Korean so they had no idea what she was saying.

CHAPTER 18

Number Twenty-Seven

Esther awoke to the jolting of the train as it stopped at their destination. A guard then opened the door to their car and a draft of frigid air even colder than Shenyang's winter winds blew in. As Esther stepped off the train, she saw a sign in the distance indicating that they were in a city in Heilongjiang Province, one of China's northernmost provinces situated on the border of Russia and Inner Mongolia. The remote area had been cut off from civilization since ancient times and, like Russia's Siberia, was the perfect place to send people the government wanted to be rid of.

Esther was led off the train still handcuffed to the North Korean woman. She was cold, hungry, and tired, but her day had just begun. She didn't have any idea what was happening or where they were going. No one told her anything and whenever she tried to ask, she was told to stop talking.

Both prisoners were put into a secure vehicle and driven to a remote prison outside of Harbin, the capital city of Heilongjiang. When they arrived at the prison gates, a guard came out to process them for entry.

Although it was definitely a prison, it was not marked with signs of any kind. The only indications of the building's grim purpose were the high walls with barbed wire, guard towers, and a tall fence surrounding the entire compound.

Esther could see that the North Korean girl was cold and hungry. When they were yanked out of the car and taken into a processing room, Esther pulled some cash out of her pocket and pleaded with the guards to buy some food for the young girl. One of the guards promptly took the money, put it in his pocket, and continued to process their paperwork. He had no intentions of using the money for their benefit.

Esther's handcuffs were taken off and she was told to undress. She did exactly as told, feeling completely humiliated and vulnerable, standing in a freezing concrete room with nothing on. A guard came and checked her over to make sure she wasn't concealing anything on her person, even combing through her hair in case something was hidden inside.

After that inspection, she was given a uniform to put on with the number twenty-seven on it. That was her new name. She was no longer Esther, but Twenty-seven.

Imprisoned Again—Underground

Soon another guard came and led her into an underground bunker in one of the special wards reserved for political criminals. The underground area was a series of mazes and reminded Esther of what she had seen in old Japanese movies.

As she walked through the series of corridors, there were cells full of women watching her as she walked by. All the women in every cell stood as close as they could to the bars in order to get a glimpse of the new girl on the block. None of them looked at her with friendliness or compassion, but instead with stoicism and indifference.

She finally arrived at her new home. The cell block doors were not automatic like in American movies, but old relics from a time long past. The big rusty doors had large keyholes and the guard carried a ring with old fashioned keys on it to open the doors. He stopped at a cell, opened it, and shoved Esther in, locking the door behind her. Esther suddenly found herself crammed into a cell with five other women, none of whom looked happy to see her. In fact, they wanted nothing to do with her.

"God, I know you are with me. I *know* you are with me, and I will not fear," she prayed to herself.

Esther stood by the door without moving for a moment. She felt awkward and didn't know how to engage the others. No one said a word.

There was no room for her to sit down, so all she could do was keep standing. After a long period of awkward silence, she decided the best thing to do was to try to be friendly and smile at them even though they were not smiling back.

"Hello," she said nervously, hoping to identify at least one other woman who would be willing to engage in niceties. No one responded. They all just stared at her. Esther tried again with the sweetest voice she could muster. "How are you?"

"What are you in here for?" one woman growled from across the cell.

"I am in here for being a Christian and for giving food to starving people." That reply got an immediate reaction from each of the ladies in the cell.

"What?" they all said in unison. "Come on! No one gets arrested for being good," said one woman.

"Yes," Esther said strongly, defending her innocence. "In fact, one of the poor young ladies I was helping is here in this prison too. She is from North Korea and the only crime she is guilty of is trying to save her own life by coming across the border to find food. My only crime was giving her that food so that she would not die."

"Sounds like those scoundrel Communists, always punishing people for anything that scares them," said one woman. With their initial suspicions assuaged, the women were immediately more receptive to what Esther had to say.

One by one they began to share with Esther about their crimes and tell her why they had been put in the women's prison.

After they had been sharing together for some time, Esther began to tell them about the love of Christ. She preached the gospel to them, unaware of the fact that they were being monitored every minute of the day. Even though the prison facilities were old and decrepit, the monitoring systems were not. The latest camera technology and microphones were used to censor everything said and done in those cells. The prison did not have heating or clean water, but they had everything necessary to eavesdrop on all of the prisoners' conversations.

Soon Esther heard a gate in the background slam hard.

The women immediately stopped talking and retreated to the back of the cell in order to distance themselves from Esther. The sound of boots marching down the hallway told everyone that trouble was coming.

A group of guards arrived at the cell.

"What are you doing, Twenty-seven? Do you think that you have come here to take a vacation?" the guard yelled. "Open this door," he demanded. Another guard nervously fumbled through his keys until he found the right one. When the door opened, the first guard lunged for Esther.

"You are not here to chat with friends. You are not here to relax. Do your time and leave." He pushed Esther up against the wall and got in her face, his spit spraying her with every syllable. "You are my prisoner and you will keep your mouth shut in my prison, Twenty-seven."

As he turned to walk away, Esther felt completely humiliated. She didn't know anyone, didn't know the rules, and didn't have any point of reference on what to do. Her world had been turned upside down and the prison officer made that painfully clear.

To make things worse, she was not even allowed to call her family to tell them where she was. In China, families are responsible to cover the expenses of their family members in prison. If an inmate needs a blanket, better food, clothing, or the like, his or her family has to pay for it. If they refuse or are unable to do so, the prisoner has to do without. Because she was not allowed to contact her family, there was no way for Esther to receive any of these necessities.

Simple Mercies

The prison cell was vile. The rats were not afraid of humans and would boldly walk around the cell as if they owned the place. The walls were covered with mold that had frozen over. Esther closed her eyes so that she didn't have to look at the filth around her.

The other women in the cell distanced themselves from Esther, probably out of fear of getting in trouble, and made her feel isolated and lonely. She couldn't sit on a bed because the beds were all taken. She couldn't sit on the floor, because it was too cold.

She couldn't even lean against the wall because it was covered with ice. She was miserable.

After she had been standing for quite some time, one of the ladies in the room lifted up her blanket and motioned for Esther to come and get in her bed to get warm. It was against prison regulations for two people to sleep under the same blanket, but this kind woman was willing to break the rules so that Esther would not freeze to death.

The lady had a soft spot for Esther. God was already showing His grace toward her. At the foot of the bed was a roll of white toilet paper, which in the prison was equivalent to gold or precious jewels. The other prisoners could not afford white toilet paper, so they had to keep reusing old rags over and over again. The lady told Esther that she could use her white toilet paper when she needed to use the restroom. It was an odd gesture, but Esther was thankful for her friendliness.

Before evening came, the signal for dinner time was given. Esther was hungry and had not eaten anything since she was arrested while cooking dinner two days prior. She was looking forward to finally getting some nourishment. Trays banged bars as food was handed through, and the sound came closer and closer. But when the food finally arrived, Esther's heart dropped. Each person's plate had only had some watery liquid swishing from side to side and one rotten turnip. Esther's turnip still had gravel on it.

She decided to forgo eating. She was hungry and wanted nothing more than to eat, but suddenly she had the urge to fast and pray. She fasted from both food and water—probably reducing shock to her system. The drinking water contained a mixture of waste and toxic lye that was constantly making the inmates sick. In order to survive, many would only drink the water that came on their dinner plate because it had been boiled and was safer to drink.

Aiding and Abetting Criminals

The next day officers came and took Esther to the interrogation ward. They tied her to a chair in such a way that no part of her body was able to move. Then they left her that way for the entire day until she was no longer able to feel her legs.

"Who is supporting you?" they asked first.

"Supporting me? No one is supporting me. I support myself."

"No, who is helping you? Who is behind your refugee operation?"

"I don't have a refugee operation. I help people who need help. I don't ask for their passports or identification."

"You are making this harder than it has to be, Twenty-seven. Stop trying to talk circles around the question by making it sound like you don't know anything. You need to start telling the truth and talking straight to us, Twenty-seven." Even though it had been a couple of days, Esther was still not used to hearing her name as a number. It seemed so impersonal and dehumanizing.

"Maybe you would like to see these," the officer said as he pulled out a record of phone calls. "We know everyone you have been talking to. Maybe you would like to enlighten us as to the nature of these phone calls…hmm?"

Esther looked down and saw all of the phone records that they had collected. The names of everyone she had called for the last couple of years were on that list, along with dates, times, and durations of each phone call.

"Are you denying that you made these phone calls?"

"No," replied Esther. "I am not denying that I made those calls. You said that, not me."

"Well, let's start on this list then. Who are these people you were talking to?"

"Some of them are relatives and others are friends."

"What did you talk about?"

"You can't possibly ask me to remember all that I talked about on those phone conversations. They were so random that I would not remember one phone call from the other," Esther said, dismissing the idea.

"Two of the people you called here are gangsters. We know that you have connections to the mob in Beijing."

"What?" Esther immediately protested. "That is not true. I don't know any gangsters and I have never worked with any gangsters as far as I know. I am a Christian." Esther could tell by the expressions on their faces that they really didn't know what she was talking about. Esther had thought she could end the conversation with one statement about being a Christian, because no honest, caring, and loving Christian would ever be mixed up with mobsters, but since the interrogators didn't really understand what "Christian" meant, it didn't help her case at all.

"We know that you have been working with mob bosses to smuggle North Korean prostitutes in and out of Shenyang," they charged.

Suddenly, it was clear that these officers had not really interrogated her neighbors and friends thoroughly. They had no idea what she was actually doing, and thought she was a human trafficker. There were so many things that they did not know and didn't understand, and Esther suddenly realized it made her situation much more serious. Because they didn't understand what it meant to be a Christian, it didn't make sense to them that anyone would just willingly help North Koreans without some sort of financial benefit. They would never believe the truth.

Esther could no longer feel her legs. The blood flow to her lower extremities was severely restricted, and her thighs were frozen to the chair and very painful. The only time she felt anything in her legs was when she tried to move them and sharp pain shot up through her hips. The same thing happened every day. From early in the morning until late at night Esther was strapped to the chair. This lasted a whole week. After that week of brutal abuse and questioning, Esther was given a sentence of two and a half years for her crime—simply summed up as aiding and abetting illegal criminals.

Esther was still not allowed to call her family or tell them where she was. She had no money to buy warm clothes or blankets and there was no one who could buy them for her. She had to completely rely on God to look after her, so she continued to fast and pray.

CHAPTER 19

Blessings Behind Bars

Awoman in the cell next to Esther's knew that she was a Christian and despised her for it. She was a tough woman with rough, course hands who reminded Esther of a field worker. She helped the warden keep order among the women inmates even though she was a prisoner herself. She watched every move Esther made and let Esther know that she would immediately report to the guards anything she did that was against the prison rules. Esther didn't know what that meant, but was not intimidated. This woman took pleasure in the knowledge that people were scared of her, delighting in their terror. And when Esther refused to be afraid, the woman was infuriated even more.

The guards relied heavily on this woman for inside information on the prisoners. In prison, information is power and the guards needed all of the information they could get in order to ensure that the system continued to run smoothly. "Listen, Christian," the woman hissed when Esther was brought back to her cell, "don't be doing any of that praying stuff in here. Do you hear me? I don't want to hear it. The prison doesn't want it either and I am going to make sure that we all get what we want."

Esther responded by bowing her head. Immediately the other woman was provoked. "Guards!" she shouted across the prison. "The Christian is praying! Twenty-seven is praying!" It sounded like the alarm of a five-year old tattling to the parents about something an older sibling had done.

Right away gates clanged and boots ran down the hall toward Esther's cell. When the two guards arrived, to the elderly woman's delight, they pulled out their clubs and began to beat Esther.

"Maybe you should pray that they will stop. Ha!" she laughed as Esther crouched under the blows. Her anger and fury were intense, but they turned to glee and satisfaction as she watched the guards beat Esther. Despite the beatings for praying, Esther couldn't do anything else. It was her automatic reaction. Whenever she had been afraid or in pain before, she knew she could always rely on Jesus.

After a while, the guards realized that they would not be able to stop her from praying by beating her, so they changed tactics. They forced her to get on her knees, put her hands on her legs, keep her back and neck straight, and look straight ahead without shutting her eyes. Whenever she would bow her head, the old woman in the next cell would shout out to the guards and they would instantly come running and punish her.

That night when Esther went to bed, her body was in so much pain that she was not able to lie down flat. The next day she decided again not to eat because she wanted to fast and pray. The more the prison guards punished her, the more she would pray. It was all she could do.

The next day, Esther noticed that the prison rules were posted on the wall of the prison. Printed in bold red letters was a rule prohibiting guards from touching any of the prisoners. Esther was blown away by this. The rule was clearly written for everyone to see.

When the guards came to her cell in the morning, they grabbed her hair as usual to haul her around like an animal, but this time she said very firmly, "Do not touch my hair."

The guard lifted his hand to hit her face for her audacity, but quickly and boldly she pointed to the sign and said, "The law of China states that you cannot abuse your prisoners. It is written right there. I didn't write it; the government leaders of China wrote it." Immediately the guard's eyes were filled with fear. He, and most of the guards, were illiterate and knew that they could be severely punished if they disregarded prison regulations and unwittingly ended up offending someone important.

Esther motioned with her hand to the guard, indicating that he should continue walking and she would follow. She needed both her hands free in order to hold up her pants that were much too big for her. As they walked through the prison corridors, Esther prayed for her own protection, but she also prayed for those around her to get saved. She began to pray for the woman who was always turning her in to the guards. She prayed that God would allow the opportunity to show her love and kindness.

Preaching in Chains

One day, Esther got her chance. She was able to strike up a conversation with the bullying old woman and shared with her about the love of Jesus. In a very short time, the hardened woman gave her heart to Christ and everything seemed to change.

Instead of reporting Esther when she prayed, the woman now joined her in prayer. Esther taught her some praise songs and they sang together in their cells. None of the prison guards were eager to do anything about it because they needed the old woman to make sure things were running smoothly in the prison. She was too valuable to the prison guards for them to offend her. From that day onward, it became clear that the guards did not want to have Esther stay much longer at the prison.

Each day of Esther's imprisonment was mentally and emotionally trying for her, especially when she learned that some of the North Koreans caught at her house in the raid had been executed by firing squad in China and the rest were sent back to North Korea where they would most likely be executed as well. It was also physically trying. The conditions at the prison seemed unbearable at times. Esther's feet were constantly cold. Several times she had to be checked for frostbite. The water in the pipes was frozen, so no one was able to bathe. The drinking water was polluted with waste chemicals. Cameras were positioned to watch their every move, even when they used the toilet.

However, in spite of the harsh conditions, each day also had its share of joyous moments. As Esther fasted and prayed, several more prisoners came to the Lord. Esther taught them about the Bible and also sang songs with them. Like Paul, she was an *"ambassador in chains"* (Ephesians 6:20). The very place she was brought to in order to prevent her from preaching the gospel became her platform for sharing about Jesus Christ.

The Holy Spirit began to work mightily in the prison. The hopeless found hope and the broken were made whole again. No one was supposed to be allowed to talk or communicate in any way, but since one of the main prison informants had now been placed in their cell, Esther and her cellmates had more privileges than the other prisoners. Because the guards were afraid of the old lady in Esther's cell who had become a believer, they left them alone.

Praying in Faith

"Esther, what are we supposed to pray about?" asked one of the younger ladies who had just received Jesus.

"Anything," she replied. "The Lord is able to hear your prayers no matter where you are. Just talk to Him. Prayer is a communication line to God. You can share your fears, desires, and troubles. He hears you and wants to build a relationship with you more than anything."

"Does He care that we don't have water?" she asked innocently.

"Yes, he cares," Esther said, knowing what was coming next.

"Can we pray for water to bathe in?"

This was truly a test. Everyone in the cell was listening. No one wanted to hear Esther explain why God couldn't or wouldn't answer their prayers. This was a time for real faith to be turned into action, and Esther didn't know how it was going to end.

"We can pray, but I can't promise that anything will happen. God said that He would give us the desires of our hearts, but our desires change when He comes into our hearts and we learn to, above all, desire to be more like Him."

"But if we become more like Jesus, will we not desire water any longer?"

"No, but let's pray together and believe that God will hear us." Esther grabbed the hands of the young lady and encouraged everyone else to hold hands as well. They prayed an earnest prayer before God and put forth a simple request to Him. Esther really didn't know what would happen. She had never prayed for water before and, in fact, had never made a prayer request for something that was not necessary for survival. Recently, the majority of her prayers were for health and freedom. She really didn't want to get beaten any more. But, she still prayed earnestly.

After they all prayed together, she walked over and turned on the tap. Warm water gushed out! Everyone was amazed. The word circulated throughout the entire prison. Esther and the other women were finally able to wash their hair.

The warmth from the water enlivened and rested Esther's entire body. Once the guards were told what had happened, they went into the cell to feel the water. To them, it felt ice cold. But to Esther and the other women, it was warm and comforting. It was a miracle for those who believed.

Transformation in the Cell

Everyone in Esther's prison cell became a Christian that day except for one. The woman who did not receive Christ was very physically imposing. Her tall stature revealed that she was definitely from northern China, as northern Chinese are much taller than their southern counterparts and have been so throughout history. Esther only came up to her armpits in height.

This woman had had a troubled childhood and had been in and out of jail since she was a teenager. She physically abused other prisoners to get what she wanted. When she wanted more food, she would just take it from others and get away with it because the other women were too weak to defend themselves.

A few days after seeing the warm water come out of the faucet she approached Esther. "Can God really hear me if I pray to Him?"

"Absolutely, you can see that He cares even about little things like warm water. Even though we may be in prison and feel like everyone has forgotten about us, I can tell you that He has never forgotten about you. He made you in His image and He loves you very much. You are His daughter and He thinks about you every moment."

She asked Esther to pray with her. When the guards saw the two of them praying, they reacted right away and yelled out for them to stop. Without thinking, Esther shouted back, "Leave us alone. We are praying!" Esther was surprised at her own reaction. She was not afraid of them any longer and had the upper hand in the prison. The longer that she was in that prison, the less control the guards had over her.

Amazed at the fact that they had warm water, the ladies came together again to pray for clean drinking water. Again, Esther wanted to teach them that God was not a genie in a bottle who just answered wishes and responded to ultimatums. "Do you believe that God can give us clean water?" asked one of the girls.

"Yes, but if not, I will still believe in Him. He has done so much for me that if He does nothing else I will still love Him. He has already given me so much. He doesn't owe me anything. However, I know that He is alive and capable. Let us pray."

After they prayed, visibly clean water that was safe to drink came out of the pipes. Everyone was amazed and loudly praised the Lord. "Your God is amazing, Esther!" one of the guards admitted upon seeing the miracle.

Her God *was* amazing, and He was working mightily in that prison through His servant Esther. The biggest miracle that happened in Esther's cell was not the clean drinking water, but the transformed lives of those imprisoned with her. Before she had arrived, the prisoners in her cell were eager to turn one another in to the guards in order to gain favor and extra privileges. No one had been loyal to anyone else. But after everyone became Christians, they loved and looked out for one another. There was a sense of duty and commitment between them that they had never experienced before.

The guards soon realized that something was different. The prisoners were less antagonistic and reports about prisoners harming other prisoners had drastically decreased. This made them very suspicious. They realized that the changed environment could lead to a revolt. They could easily control the inmates as long as they were divided against each other, but unity amongst the prisoners could lead to power struggles with the guards. They knew that

Esther was the cause of this new unity and that their top informant was now on her side. It was apparent to them that she valued Esther's friendship and approval over anything the guards could offer to her. They could not explain it, but they knew the situation was dangerous.

There was only one thing to do: get Esther out of the prison as quietly as possible. The warden was informed of the problem and Esther was called into his office. When she was brought in, he didn't make room for small talk, but got straight to the point.

"Esther, you have been brought up for parole," he said.

Esther could not believe her ears. She had only served one month of an eighteen-month sentence. She thought, *How can this be?* Tears started to form in her eyes.

"If you pay us, we will allow for your early release," the warden continued.

"But I don't have any money and my family does not even know I am here. I have no way to contact anyone to raise the money I need to be released."

The warden thought for a moment. "We will contact your family and start the process." That night Esther had a dream confirming that she would soon be released from prison.

A few days later, Esther's brother, who had government connections, arrived at the prison to pay the money required for her release. It started to snow as she walked out of the prison. As she watched it fall, she reflected on its freshness and on the tranquility of the moment. She had not seen daylight for over a month. She had been underground the entire time.

Esther breathed deeply, enjoying the air outside but not forgetting her friends inside who were now new believers and would have to continue on without a Bible or a teacher. She prayed that

God would have mercy on each one of them and lead them into fellowship with one another, searching and seeking after Him.

As Esther walked out of the main gate of the prison, her brother flagged down a taxi. They got inside, and started driving. Even as the prison faded in the distance, Esther was able to begin putting the trauma of her torturous time in prison behind her as well.

In fact, after only five minutes in the taxi, Esther had already begun to plan how to better disciple North Koreans when she returned home. A new season of ministry was about to begin.

Epilogue

After being released from prison in norther China, Esther immediately went back to serving the underground North Korean church and continued to do so for several years. That all changed when Peter, her North Korean disciple, was shot trying to cross the border between China and North Korea. The police discovered that Esther was still helping refugees, and they also uncovered a plot by the North Korean government to assassinate her. The ominous call from Peter's phone, which began our story, signaled a drastic change in Esther's entire life and ministry. It became clear that she needed to flee from her homeland as quickly as possible.

With the help of some local and foreign friends, Esther and her family were able to flee from China with the police hot on their tail. She now lives in another country where she continues to share the gospel with North Korean refugees, but is also focusing on making up for lost time with her son and husband. The long months of separation while she was in North Korea and the stressful periods of imprisonment had taken a heavy toll on the entire family, and she sees this current stage in life as a special time to invest in her husband and twentysomething son. Though her heart yearns for the salvation of the North Korean people, she fully recognizes that her current exile is a gift from God for the strengthening of her family and her physical health. Esther still has problems with her legs due to the torture she suffered in the Chinese prison and, like Paul and countless Christian martyrs before her, her body bears the marks of suffering for her Savior.

Peter, one of the many North Koreans Esther has led to the Lord, eventually recovered from his gunshot wound, was amazingly released from prison, and is now living in another country as well.

At the time of writing, Esther knows that this story must be told, but has requested that every effort be made to alter the names, places, and order of events in order to protect those involved who are still ministering to North Koreans in China. Even specific interrogation techniques used on her during her imprisonments have been left out because they might be mainly used by certain departments in specific areas that can easily be identified.

The co-author of this book has worked with Esther for several years in China and has helped to supply her with many of the audio Bibles and other materials needed for the underground church in North Korea. He was also a part of the team that helped to smuggle Peter back into North Korea prior to his arrest in China.

While being interviewed for this book, Esther asked that the following prayer requests be shared with every person who reads it:

My humble request is that you keep the dear North Korean people in your prayers.

1. Pray for the Christians who are in jail in North Korea.

2. Pray for 23,000 North Korean defectors living in South Korea who want to live Christian lives. Pray that in the future they will be able to go back to North Korea and openly share the good news and plant churches there.

3. Pray for the more than 100,000 North Korean refugees still hiding in China, that they would be safe and find salvation in Jesus.

4. Pray for those Chinese workers who are risking their lives every day to get the gospel into North Korea or who are ministering and preaching to North Korean refugees in China. Some of my family members continue to be involved in this work in my absence so your prayers for their safety and protection mean a great deal to me.

—Esther

Photos

The city of Shenyang, China, where Esther moved when she
was nineteen years old.

North Korean agriculture suffers from
years of mismanagement.

And yet its farmers and rural citizens continue to eke
out crops, still using primitive farming methods.

A typical village in North Korea

The bare mountains of North Korea.

Two of Esther's many disciples in North Korea.

Esther with North Korean officials in front of a
government building.

Esther describing her work in North Korea (top)
and her North Korean documents (bottom).